P9-CQN-322

THE PASTOR IN ACTION

THE PASTOR IN ACTION

TESTED WAYS TO MINISTERIAL SUCCESS

By

AMBROSE MOODY BAILEY

*Author of "Evangelism in a Changing World"
and "Stand Up and Preach"*

ROUND TABLE PRESS, INC.

NEW YORK   1939

PRINTED IN THE UNITED STATES OF AMERICA
BY CORNWALL PRESS, INC., CORNWALL, N. Y.

Dedicated to
All My Brother Pastors
Who Have Studied to Show Themselves
Approved unto God

CONTENTS

PREFACE

My MAIN emphasis in this volume is not on the challenge and opportunities of the Gospel ministry. That I have done in my two previous books.

Rather I have tried to make this volume a sort of practical road-map, indicating "this road is good, take it. This road is poorly graded; avoid it." It is a book of action for the younger man, and one of reflection for the older veteran in the work of the Kingdom.

My hope is that it may point out what seem to be assured stepping stones that lead one to effective service in the Gospel ministry, and to mark those which lead only to "dead ends."

For there is much joy and enriching experience in the work of the Lord, which only he who is a true shepherd of the flock can fathom and make his own. The depth of the riches of love in Christ Jesus and the joy of effective service for the Lord bring their own compensating rewards.

AMBROSE MOODY BAILEY.

Lowell, Mass.

I

CALLED TO THE GOSPEL MINISTRY

To EVERY one called into the Gospel Ministry there comes a moment of reflection. To such a one—or to such a group, the discussion inevitably turns to a consideration of the minister; how he came to be, who he is, and what he is expected to accomplish in his divine calling with his feeble, finite, human limitations.

On one of these occasions, Father Manion of the Catholic rectory across the street from me, gave voice to an analysis of the Christian ministry, which I believe will bear repeating not only for those in the ministry, but for those laymen and women who hold up our arms in the service of the Lord. I quote it because it gives an insight into the work of the true servant of the Living God:

> I am an average pastor—a misunderstood individual, at least I think so. People suspect me of being a little more than human, but continue to invite me to eat their dinners at their homes. If I come, they call me a good fellow. If I refuse, they say I'm stuck up.

> They expect me to have no faults whatsoever, and then keep on searching for them. When they discover any—Oh, boy!

> When I haven't prepared my talk, and my mind is cloudy and my ideas chaotic, they say I'm too deep; when I labor with zeal, and have my thoughts properly presented, they say I'm superficial.

When my decks are clean financially, and I'm not over my head in debts, then I'm a grafter. If my books wouldn't balance, and I were in the red, then I'd be a poor business man. If I remind them to keep their church contributions paid to date, then I'm always preaching about money. And if I don't, and the church year ends with just a few unpaid bills, then I'm a failure, and am slipping badly.

If I shake the hands of some dear old lady too long, I'm sentimental. If I don't shake hands at all, I'm devoid of human feeling, and am lacking in sentiment.

When my liver is out of order, and I am physically ill and mentally tired, they say I look pious and saintly. When I am well and bubbling all over with zeal, they hint that I am rather frivolous.

They think I should like everyone in the city; and when I try my best to run counter to nature, they say I'm a hypocrite. If I honestly admit there are some I am not enthusiastic about, they call me a snob.

Folks who are comfortably fixed financially find fault with me if I do not call on them; those who are poor find fault if I do.

Some people in my presence pretend to be keenly interested in everything that pertains to religion. They minimize my intelligence and exaggerate their own stage ability.

Generous contributors pity me because I have such a hard time getting the amount of money I need to carry on the work which means so much to me and to my parish. Stingy souls are convinced that I have an extremely soft job.

Some wonder what I do with all my time, others pity me because I have so much to do.

They want me to be more of a layman and to represent them in civil and public activities, but they are forever praising another because he is so quiet and retiring and is such a holy man.

If I use forceful and catchy phrases in my talks, I'm trying to be sensational. If I don't catch their attention, their heads may nod, and they may fall asleep.

Stockbrokers must think I'm a millionaire—at least judging by the amount of circular mail they send me; book agents think I'm easy; tramps KNOW that I am.

If the world should ask me, I'd like to say:

That my title doesn't change my human nature. I am quite the same as other men are, in my human reactions.

That I too enjoy a legitimate good time, just as much as any of them; but I prefer to choose my own kind of sport or recreation.

That I have had to train myself to grow immune to knocks and criticism; if I hadn't, it would be just too bad for me.

That I can spot flattery and "soft soap" a mile away. But I do appreciate like every one else honest praise, and desire no man's pity.

That I am endeavoring to give to my work the very best that is in me; and I have faith in God that He will reward me in His own Way.

That I want no favors and seek only the opportunity to show that I am a real man and want to be a faithful Servant of the Living God and a friend to all mankind.

Even now I know that some are thinking that I get my ideas from others; and so I do!

THE CHRISTIAN PASTOR—A TEN-SIDED MAN

Let's face this subject honestly and frankly, for in spite of all of our own human reactions, we do seek to live a life worthy of our best. As I see it, the Christian pastor to succeed in his calling today, must be a ten-sided man.

1. He is a man, a human being with needs, feelings and normal reactions. It is therefore important that he keep well, that he pay his debts, and that he live a life worthy of himself and of God, a life above all human reproach. Consequently it is extremely important to a minister that he choose a help-meet from those of good health, and from a family whose moral standing in the community is above reproach. She should possess a good mental grasp, a pure soul, a devotion to religion, and a keen interest in religious practices. She should be a neat housekeeper, devoid of a nature tending toward jealousy or suspicion. She must not be quick tempered, nor have a tongue that runs to babbling. She must be frugal, and show a tendency to be careful in financial matters. She ought never to be a restive spirit. Perhaps it should be said that a minister ought to marry as nearly an ideal woman as is possible. Eliza Harvey of the Second Church, Chicago, offers with sardonic exactitude these qualifications for the wife of a successful minister these days:

> "Wanted a perfect lady,
> Delicate, gentle, refined—
> With every beauty of person
> And every endowment of mind;
> Fitted by early culture
> To move in fashionable life.
> Please notice our advertisement,
> 'Wanted, a minister's wife.'

Wanted, a thoroughbred worker,
Who, well to her household looks;
(Shall we see our money wasted
By extravagant, stupid cooks?)
Who cuts the daily expenses
With economy sharp as a knife,
And washes and scrubs in the kitchen;
'Wanted, a minister's wife.'

A very domestic person;
To callers she must not be 'out,'
It has such a bad appearance
For her to be gadding about.
Only to visit the parish
Every year of her life,
And attend the funerals and weddings,
'Wanted, a minister's wife.'

To conduct the ladies' meetings,
The sewing circle attend;
And when we work for the needy,
Her ready assistance to lend.
To clothe the destitute children
Where sorrow and want are rife;
To hunt up Sabbath-school scholars,
'Wanted, a minister's wife.'

Careful to entertain strangers,
Traveling agents and such;
Of this kind of 'angel visits'
The leaders have had so much
As to prove a perfect nuisance,
And 'hope these plagues of their life
Can soon be sent to their parson's—
'Wanted, a minister's wife.'

A perfect pattern of prudence,
To all others spending less,
But never disgracing the parish
By looking shabby in dress;
Playing the organ on Sunday
Would aid our laudable strife
To save the society's money—
'Wanted, a minister's wife.' "

2. He has a big business—the business of saving souls. He must have the proper equipment, and so he has an office, where he receives and answers correspondence, where he keeps some of it filed for convenient reference; and where he receives those who come to him for advice, help and inspiration. Here too he must compose sermons, read, plan his programs, and do a thousand and one tasks which come to him for direction, consideration and decision.

3. He has a relationship to multitudes of folk as their friend and spiritual counsellor. When they are sick, he visits them, and comforts them. He holds their secrets inviolate. When they are in need of food and clothing, he must see that they are aided. When they have particular joy, he must share it with them. He must be their friend in every social occasion.

4. He is a citizen of a commonwealth. He must pay his taxes when they are due. He must pay his bills like others, except that he must pay them more promptly. He must keep in touch with political issues. He must be a voter in the elections. He must perform his duty as a well informed voter on every important issue, but must restrain himself from becoming a partisan.

5. He is a member of a denominational group. He will honor with respect his ranking officers, and maintain a fraternity of spirit with confreres. He must wherever possible

serve on boards and committees, and attend and speak often as a delegate at conventions and assemblies. He must do as much of this larger work as may be possible consistent with the needs of his own parish. There must be a proper balance.

6. He is the one man who sees the parish whole. Under his jurisdiction, every need must have its place. In his mind its entire pattern is televisualized.

7. He is a member of the Kingdom of God. As such he has a genetic relation to every other Church or religious agency in his city and in the world, regardless of shade of faith or creed. He must be a true witness for the Kingdom of God, and as such, men must know where he stands, even though often he must let his silence speak.

8. His Church must have funds with which to carry on the work of the parish. He must be a shrewd financial adviser, and a wise administrator.

9. He was ordained to perform certain ceremonies: funerals, weddings, baptisms, dedications; all demand his time and attention. He must have the proper attitudes toward each.

10. He must be a man of character and education. The real test of education is character, for intelligence is more than book knowledge. In a day of intellectual unrest and social ferment the educated pastors—those trained in colleges and seminaries and possessing character not copied from books— are a bulwark of the Church, steering it away from transitory ism, schism and spasm.

If a man possesses these qualifications, he has a foundation on which a successful pastorate can be built.

It will be, always, to the advantage of the pastor if in his youth he has been reared in the Christian Church, nurtured by godly parents, and ingrafted in the method of Church life, early enough that its technique is a common and normal practice of his life. This is a groundwork of education in the ministry which will continuously express itself in his work.

It will be a further advantage if the pastor may have had some commercial experience in his youth, or at least have had practice in the actual business of church management early in his career; or failing in that, that he serve an interneship as an assistant under an older pastor preferably in a large church where the business of church management counts in the work of the church parish.

THE OLDEST TEXTBOOK FOR PASTORS

Leviticus, of the Old Testament, can rightfully be called the oldest book known, dealing with the pastoral office. It is not, I will concede, an interesting book even to preachers. Leviticus has within it little to inspire the casual reader: it is less interesting even than a denominational Book of Discipline or a Service Book to the layman. But to a consecrated minister of the Gospel, who evaluates his divine calling, Leviticus is full of inspiration and direction.

The treatise of Leviticus begins with minute directions for five different types of Tabernacle or Temple offerings: the burnt offering, the meat (meal) offering, the peace offering, the sin offering, the trespass offering. It is followed by directions as to how the priests as a social group were to be supported; for since society needed their ministrations, they must be fed, clothed and cared for. It was of great importance that the priest felt his own self-respect as well as maintained the self-respect of the community which he served.

Laws, too, are included in Leviticus for the consecration of priests. Their individual character must be above reproach. It is interesting to read the story of Nadab and Abihu, sons of Aaron, which the author of Leviticus feels so important that he goes afield to tell the story. When Nadab and Abihu lost their character, they lost their lives; and none mourned them.

In reading Leviticus we must bear in mind that these pages of the Holy Bible were intended for that time. To make its rules applicable to today's conditions would be an anachronism. Even in the tenth chapter of The Acts of the Apostles we read how some of these ancient laws were later abrogated.

Here in Leviticus there are hygienic provisions for women; rules for the care of leprosy and uncleanness. Even in those days men realized that religion and the betterment of human society were inter-related, and were of vital significance to each other.

The problem of how to deal with the individual who suffers from a guilty conscience is spread within the pages of Leviticus. Holidays are authorized in Leviticus, perhaps to indicate to the pastors that holidays do have their place in their work also. Leviticus authorizes five of them. One of the strangest of these observances is the Old Testament provision for a year of Jubilee every fifty years, in which debts were to be forgiven and the slaves manumitted. This observance seems to suggest a day when a better social order would prevail, and men would be freed from the human bondage, they may have gotten themselves into.

Leviticus can become an interesting book for the pastor.

ASPIRATION AND IDEALS

The pastor, perhaps more than any one in other occupational pursuits, must seek inspiration far and wide. Many pastors have drawn much inspiration from a study of paintings, particularly those of the old masters.

At least once in his life every pastor must make a pilgrimage to Boston, to see there at the Boston Public Library at Copley Square, those great expressions of art given to the world by John Singer Sargent and Edwin Abbey, whose masterpieces comprise *The Quest of the Holy Grail*. Often have I drunk in at this fount of great inspiration—as have many others who have gone to Boston to see them; for in these enriching paintings one will find *the first formula for all pastoral labor*.

You know the story behind these paintings. The Holy Grail was fabled to be the sacred vessel from which our Lord Jesus Christ had drunk at the Last Supper, and the vessel into which Joseph of Arimathea is said later to have gathered the blood coming from His wounds.

The Holy Grail awaited the coming of the perfect knight. It possessed the power to make such a one know and live. But only one who was pure in heart and life could touch it and grasp the Holy Grail. The entire series of Edwin Austin Abbey's *The Quest of the Holy Grail* is shown in fifteen scenes on the entablature of an upper room.

The first painting of the series pictures the child Galahad being visited by an angel carrying the Holy Grail. In the second painting, the child, now grown, is being girt for going forth on the quest; in the third, he sits in the seat that awaits a blameless occupant. In the fourth, he sets forth on his great adventure. The fifth scene—this is the most famous of the entire series—is on the North Wall and occupies the entire upper part of the end of the room.

Visitors from all parts of the world have felt the inspiration of this great painting in the light of its perfect coloring, its form and symbolism. Here Amfortas, King of the Grail, is helpless under a spell. All the inmates of the castle are spiritually dead. The Holy Grail is there, but those who are present cannot see it. No one can be liberated from this condition of bondage until the great knight, pure in heart and in life, comes and through the influence of the Holy Grail, restores unto them life and radiant joy. Sir Galahad believes it is he who can save these men. The Holy Grail floats before him in all its awe-inspiring splendor. He has only to take it and speak deliverance to them. He reaches for the Holy Grail. And lo! like Tennyson after Hallam's death:

> "I stretch vain hands of faith and grope,
>   and gather dust. . . ."

Nothing had happened. Sir Galahad spoke, but his speech had no liberating power. These suppliants, the dead and the damned, still are before him helpless. The Holy Grail has disappeared. What was amiss? One thing only, and that was within his own soul: his own heart was not right toward God. The weary trek must be begun again.

Sir Galahad rides forth from the castle, and a roar of despair rises like thunder behind him. The needy souls curse him for his failure and lack of preparedness. The earth, weary with its own heavy sorrows and older sin, must endure another baptism in tears until the day when the Perfect Knight shall come.

JOHN SINGER SARGENT

Upstairs also in the Boston Public Library, on the third floor, you will find John Singer Sargent's *Frieze of the Prophets*. This great painting portrays a general history of religion, starting when religion was but a darkened impulse in the mind of man. The artist traces it graphically through its various revelations, coming on to the Hebrew faith. Here he shows Moses, the giver of the law, and the start of the order of priesthood. Then he pictures the prophets in turn. A vacant panel remains where, had the artist lived, Sargent would have painted Jesus Christ seated on one of Galilee's lovely hillsides. The final thought of the series is that of Jesus's death and the empty tomb, indicative of His Triumph. Here is the Savior, but bound with Him upon His cross are Adam and Eve, typifying humanity. They are man's representatives. The artist seems to hint that Jesus can never come down from His cross until suffering society also comes down from its cross of suffering. The objective of salvation is a redeemed society and the promised coming of the Kingdom of God.

*   *   *   *   *

These thoughts of purity and social redemption are the major ones on which Leviticus is built concretely. Be right with God. Bring righteousness to men. One is profoundly impressed with this thought when reading this book of Leviticus. More than 3,000 years ago the office of spiritual oversight had already become formulated into prescribed principles and practices. It had already become a discipline and an art.

Against such a background one is prepared to read the scathing words of Jeremiah and Ezekiel. "Who are these," these words seem to say, "who have made this their great life-work, but who have bungled it so badly." The priests of their days are held up for our condemnation because they were men without adequate spritiual perception, and because they pretended to mediate God merely as a means for obtaining profitable revenue.

In contrast, the pastor who has thoroughly consecrated himself and who has dedicated his life to the great objective of salvation, knows the depth of meaning in these words:

> "But none of the ransomed ever knew,
> How deep were the waters crossed;
> Nor how dark was the night that the Lord passed through,
> E're he found his sheep that was lost."

THE PASTOR'S ORDINATION

After the theological student has completed his years of adequate preparation, he presents himself for ordination. In different Church groups different methods prevail. But when the candidate for ordination presents himself, his thoughts are not on the many sermons he must preach, but with the call of the Master: "I have chosen you and *ordained you.*" (John 15:16)

In many Churches this examination for ordination takes place before larger groups from the congregation or before smaller committees of fellow-ministers.

Questions are asked of the candidate. In place of the often-asked questions in previous periods—those dealing with Inspiration of the Scriptures, the Miracles, the Virgin Birth, and the Atonement—the candidate nowadays is more likely to be asked rather pointedly: "Are you a socialist?" "Do you believe in the equal distribution of wealth?" "Do you object to our present social order?"

After the council is convinced that the candidate has had adequate and well-grounded training and has reached wholesome Christian convictions based on the great teachings of Jesus, the council goes into executive session, and probably brings in a report of acceptancy. Its recommendation for approval and ordination is usually accepted by the congregational group, even though many will wish to defer their vote until they have expounded and defended their own particular shibboleth. Should the candidate have a particular friend or relative present in the executive session, it would be thoughtful if that friend or relative spoke and insisted upon a complete, unqualified approval of the candidate, so that no evasive or half way motion is permitted to be presented or passed. When all are satisfied with the candidate's conversion and the sincerity of his divine call to the Christian ministry, the candidate is ordained to that high and holy office, according to the services required by that Church.

THE FIRST CALL TO PARISH SERVICE

The qualities which should be sought for by the Church who wishes to call the pastor are:

1. The candidate must be a follower of the Christ.
2. He must be able to preach the Gospel acceptably.
3. He must have social gifts which enable him to meet people and help them.

4. He must have ability to deal tactfully with men and women, and to do it with Christian poise.
5. He must be a leader, with courage to lead.

Other qualifications will be added by others who have in mind particular conditions which the candidate will have to face in his first or later parishes.

There are many ways in which the candidate may be called to his first field—the greater number of these are legitimate and fair. The dean of the theological seminary usually is consulted, and in other cases the denominational head of that area is asked for recommendation of a pastor, or he offers to recommend several possible candidates. Laymen, too, have a part in the selection of possible candidates, especially those who attend regularly the annual meetings of their Church group, for they have a wider acquaintance with possible candidates than other church officers may have.

THE ABUSE OF THE CALL

That there is abuse of the call to service, no one will deny. Far too often a pastorless church will seek another pastor from a larger field of service, and offer great inducements prior to his acceptance of the call. Churches have sought successful men, or younger men of charm and great personality—it is such a human failing—without considering the needs of the parish. Is the call to a Christian Church parish to be considered on the elements of salary, prestige or material "offers"? or is the first need that should be considered that of the spiritual needs of the parish? Has a church a right to disturb a man who is doing an outstanding work for the Lord, and who is happily at work in his section of the great Vineyard?

Should the call be unanimous? By all means, or if not, those who extend the call should be frank and honest enough to say that there is a considerable group of the parish who will be set in opposition to the new pastor from the start. The pastorate is difficult enough under any given conditions without this additional handicap.

Suppose though that the candidate should be unfortunate enough to be called into a situation where there is considerable opposition to his coming—of which he had not previously been aware. In that case he should not get discouraged and lose his self-control in any way. He should make it his first business to exercise Christian love and to cultivate and win over the larger number of those who through misunderstanding may have been opposed to his coming. Many cases there are on record where such opposition has been won over, and it has become in time a bulwark for aggressively fruitful work in that parish. Remember that many of these Sauls have become the Pauls of our modern church life.

GETTING OFF TO A RIGHT START

What should the new pastor do before he begins work in his new field of service? What type of information should he request, so that no time will be lost and so that he will be enabled to assume his role of pastor more quickly in the new parish. In most cases the information indicated below, is readily given upon request:

1. From the treasurer or financial secretary, detailed information about the current operating budget.

2. From the Sunday School superintendent or secretary, an up-to-date compilation of all members according to departments, particularly the names and addresses of those who are not already members of the Church.

3. From the Church secretary, a copy of each weekly church bulletin. If the minutes of the various meetings or those of the organizations could be obtained, they will be most enlightening and helpful.

4. From the Church Treasurer or Secretary, a typed copy of the last annual meeting, with all appended annual reports including that from the Treasurer.

5. From the Church Secretary, a printed or typewritten copy of the constitution or bylaws under which the Church operates.

6. From the most active layman, or officer, a detailed account of how the services have been conducted under former pastorates, particularly an account of the way in which the Lord's Supper has been observed in the latest pastorate.

7. From the Sunday School superintendent or from a department head, some idea as to general plans for the observance of special Sundays, etc.

8. From the President of the Women's Society, an informative letter or samples of materials which will help to orientate the new pastor with its work.

9. From miscellaneous sources: A copy of the marriage laws of the state; a pocket-size map of the city; names and addresses of those who serve the church commercially—the printer, florist, funeral director, etc.

10. If the Church has a paid or volunteer Secretary, suggest that she have ready a 4 x 6 file card giving the following information on the Church membership: (The information required on such a printed file card will vary considerably in many cases from that which I have included on the card on page 18. The information may be mimeographed or multigraphed on the card with just as effective a result. But unless the card has on it exactly the type of information which the

pastor needs, it does not serve its full purpose. Remember that the time of the Church secretary is precious, too.)

NAME	Male	
	Female	
Occupation	Home Address	Res. Tel.
Resident	Business Address	Bus. Tel.
Non Resident		
Active		
Inactive		

Number in Family	Joined Church by Baptism, Letter, Relation, Restoration
Names Ages S.S.Ch.M.	Joined Church (Date)
	Is a contributor of record to Current expenses
	Is contributor to Missions
	Attends Church regularly
	Attends S.S. regularly
	Attends Prayer Meeting regularly
	Date of Birth or approximate age
	Last recorded attendance at Communion
Remarks:	

To a newly-appointed pastor, requesting this information from his new parish in advance of his coming, such information may seem premature. But after years of experience, he will readily agree that such a list will always be invaluable. He will tend to request much more detailed information then than has been here indicated.

At any rate, it will give the new congregation the feeling that he "means business," and that he is determined to become informed on all phases of their work at the earliest possible moment. It will save much time and indicate a proper enthusiasm for the work of the parish that shall soon have his oversight.

Let me pause here just long enough to drop an important hint. Ascertain tactfully but accurately the list of the names and tenure of office, by years, of the former ministers in that parish. Suppose, for an illustration, the shortest pastorate was for six months and the longest was for eight years. Suppose that in 126 years the church has had twenty-seven pastors. In that case the average tenure of office was five years. Compare then the last few pastorates with that average, and see if those pastorates were longer or shorter than the average. The feeling of restiveness is ingrained in American life. Was the restlessness with the church or with the pastor? Such a study will be particularly enlightening. It may indicate just what tendencies to guard against, if one is to remain long in that field.

BE HONEST IN YOUR SERMONS

It may seem like a truism to say that whatever one says, one must be original. The story has been told me of a young man of promise who found a splendid, inspiring sermon copyrighted by a pastor in Nashville, and who delivered it with the full force of his personality. "That boy has great promise" commended the older people of the church. "He's one of us and speaks our language," enthused the youngsters.

A year went by, and at the State Rally he heard the same address almost word for word delivered again by his classmate, Brown. No one seemed to notice this, excepting himself. But it did trouble him. The following morning the local newspaper printed the sermon in its entirety. Later on, the newspaper served him with papers for violation of the copyright laws, since they in turn had been sued by the publishers. He confessed, and consulted with the Dean of his theological seminary. The matter was hushed up, and the suit was dropped; but he decided to heed the lesson, and to preach his own thoughts no matter how poorly he was able to express them.

The point he always remembered was to give proper credit as to the source of the material he used word for word from another. Illustrations however are generally considered common property.

II

A RIGHT START

THE pastor, after accepting the call to his new parish, will time his arrival at the field. Not on a Monday, for everyone seems too busy on Monday. Not on a Saturday either, for that day does not provide enough time for orientation. The best day seems to be the day on which is held the mid-week service. In the middle of the week most of the scheduled necessities seem to have been provided for.

As the new pastor nears the station he will feel a surge of homesickness and a sense of stage fright. These feelings will soon pass. The scene at the station is accurately predictable. The chairman of the Pulpit Committee will be there with his wife. The gathering will include as many of the important people as the church possesses. Cars will be waiting, and all the people will be expectant.

The greeting of the men will be jovial. Within the first five minutes one will have met the men who control the destiny of a church and that of the pastor, too. Here are usually the chairmen of all important boards of the church. Just a hint: if one has a recognized social emblem for wearing in the lapel of his coat, this is the time to wear it. The fraternal hand is outstretched, and a friendly voice welcomes you: "George!"

PRESENTATION OF LETTERS

It usually takes a moment to pass over to the Clerk, the church letters of transfer for pastor and wife, and to give a few congratulatory messages from well-known people. Courteous overtures from the former parish are a part of every transfer. Here may be letters from the Dean or College President, the Mayor of one's home city, and others in the public eye. These letters of appreciation and commendation pave the way to friendship and understanding in the new parish.

I would always recommend that the first few days of the new pastor's arrival be spent in a local hotel. Excellent rooms at reduced rates are available while one looks around unhampered for a house in which to live and work. Count the church fortunate that does not own its own parsonage!

PARSONAGES? NO!

Parsonages are never adjustable in size to one's family needs, and a location that suits one man will irk another. Moreover, the furniture it contains is often a worn-out carry-over of another's taste, and it is impossible either to keep it up to date or to discard it. Be sure to take ample time to decide and secure just the dwelling that fits into your plans and temperament.

Among the very first things to do, after the dwelling has been chosen, is to make a hurried inspection of the church roll. It is expedient to familiarize one's self with the names of the church at the earliest possible moment. Available, almost at once then, must be this roll or card index to the membership, so that it can be secured and studied. Be careful never to offer as an alibi: "I never could remember names," or to hope to get by, telling the story of the negro who "knew the face, but couldn't organize it." In the ministry one *must* have a photographic memory, at least for names and faces.

THE FIRST MEETING

If the above recommendations are carried out, then the first meeting at which the new pastor is to appear will be the mid-week service. It has its defined pattern. Brevity, not to exceed an hour in length; hymns of a spirited quality or those particularly familiar to the new congregation; a responsive reading, expressing hope—"The Lord is my strength and my Redeemer"; a prayer; and an opportunity for testimony.

Prepare a brief talk on prayer and its value and importance in human life. "Behold he prayeth" (Acts 9:11) was the proof even long ago that Paul was genuine. Sincere longing for God finds expression in prayer. The new pastor will lead in prayer and suggest that others follow his lead. He will explain that he rarely calls persons by name to lead in prayer. Personal prayer, to be real, must be voluntary. Group praying of prayers like "Our Father" is different. Let them sing another hymn with which they are all familiar. Ask if there are any sick who should be reported upon, and then close the meeting. The closing will be simple. Ask them to stand; start to sing "Blest be the tie that binds." They will readily join it. Ask them to pray together the familiar petition beginning: "Let the words of my mouth and the meditations of my heart be acceptable in thy sight, Oh Lord, my Strength and my Redeemer." Recite it in unison.

While all are still bowed in prayer, say softly: "It is our first service together. Let us feel its unity. Let us join hands in a circle around the vestry for the benediction. After you have been dismissed, stop at the door to greet me. Perhaps also tonight you will wish to shake hands with someone here whom you do not know already. I hope so."

There will greet you at the door, as you suggest, almost the entire group that were at the station. You will be surprised to discover how many of them you can recall by name and face.

Friday morning the Chairman of the Visitation Committee may come for you in his car. Spend that entire day, calling upon the aged and those seriously ill or who are shut-in. Visit also the local hospital, and become acquainted with its heads. This visit will serve an added purpose: it will familiarize one's mind also with the town. During the course of the day one may meet at least twenty families—say four each hour.

On Saturday morning let someone else answer all telephone calls for you, if possible. Remain at your desk uninterrupted for the entire day in final preparation for your first Sunday sermon. Preparation for it is very essential, for the people will come to hear you, and may be led to form their opinion of you at that time. First impressions last. In these hours you will have prepared in final form three addresses; a morning sermon with the general title "My First Sermon," a men's class talk, and an evening address.

One too must quickly come to terms with the Sunday School lesson. Many schools are no longer using the International Lessons. Much graded material now in use is advanced sufficiently for easy adaptation to adult needs. By way of getting started, why not turn to the general subject of

"The Bible Itself." Give that first Sunday, a rapid, popular analysis of some one book of the Bible. Try to provoke an interest in daily devotional reading of the Bible. Men always show interest in a fresh presentation of the Bible, or in a discussion of any popular event or topic when the light of the Cross or the Bible falls full upon it.

THE EVENING SERVICE

The evening sermon must be quite different. For a definite idea, tell the story of the day in which you met and talked with Helen Keller. In a high yet husky, falsetto voice she said with face aglow, "I—am—happy." Here is your cue. Wherein lies the secret of happiness? Find an answer in the Beatitudes and in Jesus', "If ye know these things happy are ye if ye do them." Happiness is the bluebird that will pick crumbs only from the hand of moral obedience. That seizure upon subjects of popular interest for the evening should be cultivated and it will bring returns. You have met Richard Byrd, or Einstein, or George Bernard Shaw, or Roosevelt, or Lindbergh, or Paderewski or Benes, deposed from Czecho-Slovakia. "And a greater than Solomon is here." Watch for these popular opportunities and capitalize them.

THE NUT

Sudden interruptions are the common lot of all down-town services. He wanders in, with soiled collar and unkempt hair. The pastor and the head usher are the only ones to note his presence. He waits until the service is well on its way, then rises dramatically, and pointing a skinny finger asks: "What do you believe about the sleep of the dead?" or it may be socialism, or Russia, or Saturday as a day of worship, or the Mayor of the city whom he qualifies and labels.

The incident is taking the measure on both minister and people. Will you be discerning? Or sympathetic? Or severe? Or unjust? Or frightened? Or perturbed? Can one refrain from communicating panic to such an assembly? Theodore Roosevelt controlled the situation when a crank shot him in the side, in the city of Milwaukee. Take careful measure of your own stride: "My brother wishes to know my views about the resurrection of the dead. It is a proper question; and if he will please be seated for the moment, until I have finished with my sermon, I shall be most happy to answer him at any length."

Turn to the man and say, "Thank you, my brother, for seating yourself. I see that you have the instincts of a gentleman."

The enquirer waits a moment like the lions in Clyde Beattie's cage; sits down bewilderedly, and the pastor says to the audience with a smile, "All men such as he, are my friends."

A ripple of amused astonishment passes over the congregation. They know that the service is in the hands of a master. This is a technique that never fails. One can always call the police, but the meeting has been disrupted.

FIRST SERMON—THE ART OF LEADERSHIP

One's first sermonic pulpit approach to a new or strange congregation should be considered not as an exercise in preaching, but as an effort to sense what the pastoral relationship there demands. Certain subjects are excluded. Money? Of course not. It must be upon some broad, central declaration calculated to bring the maximum good to the greater number of believers.

Here is one man's evaluation of his own work on that occasion. He chose for his text Job 22:21, "Acquaint now thyself with him and be at peace; thereby good shall come unto thee." He told his congregation why he chose that. His father had a favorite story of an old circuit rider in the country who never preached from any other text. "If one man could preach all his life from one text surely I can do it once," he thought to himself.

His sermon had four divisions; first, acquaintance with God is the most important quest of the human soul. Second, it may be attained only by an acquaintance through Jesus. He spoke rapidly and did not pause to elaborate. The audience glimpsed what he was trying to say.

"This is life eternal, that they might know thee, the only true God, and Jesus Christ." "For God, who commanded the light to shine out of darkness, hath shined in our hearts, to give the light of the knowledge of the glory of God in the face of Jesus Christ."

Third, the result of such acquaintance with God through Christ is peace. And, the fourth, the urgency to do it now. As in all preaching, he developed the sermon so that it would lead to a practical conclusion in which the hearer is asked to do something definitely about it.

Let us consider that sermon of his. If one were preaching a first sermon would he use that text? No. The text is in the Old Testament, and is not in its best known book. He might choose to speak on Jesus, or faith, or prayer, or on the values inherent in the Christian Life, or on the Cross and its challenge, or on the Christian Church and its place in the world, or on the task directly ahead. But his text voices a false philosophy. It was spoken by Eliphaz the Temanite. It cannot be maintained that allegiance to God will always give peace in this world. With Jesus it meant a cross. For a thousand martyrs it has meant death. Or what is its meaning for confessional Christians in German Concentration Camps, in 1939.

1. *A first sermon must always exalt Christ.* A minister is like a lover. She sees her beloved everywhere. Here is a rich and eccentric old lady whom it will not do to ignore, asking the new pastor to preach on the text Josh. 9:5 "Old shoes and clouted upon their feet."

Mrs. Inheritance Penny has grown up in that church. Her father has given the organ and several of the memorial windows. The text with her is the test she applies to every preacher. If he can preach on that text he will do. The congregation know well what is coming and are inwardly casting lots on how the event will turn out. Mrs. Penny has her pastor against the door jamb with the yardstick, carefully taking his height. The verse will not present great difficulties. It is the story of those Gibeonite cowards whose unworthy action betrayed them into endless servitude as "hewers of wood and drawers of water" because they knew no Savior. It paints the results of sin.

> "Tomorrow and tomorrow and tomorrow,
> Creeps in its petty pace from day to day
> To the last syllable of recorded time.
> And all our yesterdays have lighted fools,
> The path to dusty death."

But not so the feet of the righteous. "How beautiful upon the mountains are the feet." Pause to let the choir sing it. The congregation will sing:

> "Take my hands and let them move
> At the impulse of thy love.
> Take my feet and let them be
> Swift and beautiful for thee."

The congregation enjoys such an interruption. Read them Ephesians 6:15. "Our feet shod with the preparation of the gospel of peace." Also read them the First Psalm.

Pick up the thought of the sermon again. Put the unwashed feet of the disciples into the hands of the master on that last night of the Cross, while the mire of the world is laved away. Remember, no playacting. Be sincere!

Here is a text without a word of the New Testament in it; yet when the hour is over, men and women may be found treading a blood-sprinkled way following feet that have been pierced.

Sermons, too, must be preached dealing with a warless world, a more just economic order, pure government and a better relation between the races of the world. But these things do not suggest themselves. Each one of them may be related to the program of Jesus. They are hitched to the purpose of an incarnate God who bids us shoulder a Cross.

2. *A first sermon must be always practical.* Readers of Pearl Buck's stories will remember that she shows that China has always believed the world peopled with demons. One does not raise a finger in China, that they do not touch one of them. Perhaps we do, too, but ours is done according to scientific findings. Witness the man who coughed in our

face, and consequently we too had a roughness of the throat. Another one has a father who is profane and abusive. Another has insanity in the blood stream and ought never to marry. These problems press on us like demons. Here is a mother who is only twenty-three years of age, and has children five and six years of age. She is separated from the children's father, and she is now working to maintain her family, for a garage owner, who exacts from her too heavy a moral toll. Another victim of this social maladjustment comes to ask for rent money or for an old suit of clothing. Disease, loneliness, want, temptation, social pressure, spring out at us from all sides. Others tell falsehoods about us. Our own children make hideous and embarrassing mistakes. The mills shut down. Stevenson was not the first or the last to say: "Satan met me." How do the irreligious live? "If the righteous scarcely be saved where shall the ungodly and the sinner appear?" We must take man as he is, and try to make him over in God's Image.

Our missionaries see this task so much more clearly than we do. Here is a poor fellow who starts on his pilgrimage to find peace. It is not in the kiss that he places on the bronze, unresponsive toe of his god Buddha. He journeys to the blue ice caves of the upper passes of the Himalayas bordering on Tibet, and gazes long upon those phallic symbols. He comes away even from there as he went, with an oppressive foreboding heavy upon him. He hastens to the sacred Ganges, and drinks and bathes praying for cleansing, while the charred bodies of the dead float by. But there on the very banks of the Ganges, are the missionaries of the Christ who tell of a God of Love, not a devil of justice. They tell of a Christ who demands no compensation, but Who gives freely His forgiveness, urging the weary traveler to cast his heavy, sin-burdened heart upon the everlasting mercy of a God of Love, and find rest for his soul.

3. *The first sermon must be evangelical.* Mohammed's dying question was, "Have I ever failed any of you?" We as preachers of the Gospel can stand boldly and declare a Christ who never fails. We must bring Jesus to the frightened rowers in the fourth watch in the night and say assuringly to them, "It is the Lord." That night of fear and uncertainty still rests heavily upon a darkened world.

One's pastoral work may be said to have begun at the close of that first sermon. The closing hymn has been sung, and the benediction pronounced. Two people hurry down the aisle to say, "You may send for our letters of transfer." Thereafter, it is easy to say, "If there are those of you who would see me on any matter, please wait for me at your right-hand side of the pulpit. Especially do I make this suggestion to you who are considering the Christian life or membership in this Christian Church. I will see you as soon as possible after I have greeted the other folk at the door." And do it quickly, too.

It will come to be an accepted procedure. And many will come who would not have come otherwise. There are thousands of people outside our churches who would come tomorrow if they knew where to find the latch on the door. Why not leave the door that opens to a Christian acceptance slightly ajar?

BE A GOOD LISTENER

After the service several invitations to dine may be extended, and one accepts them though one may prefer to dine alone. Partake of food sparingly. This caution will give the more time to guide the conversation and to observe—and it may save you nervous indigestion! Keep a record book of all such invitations, and scrupulously repay in kind.

Twenty minutes after the serving of the meal is long enough to remain. "I must scratch a little more this afternoon if I would feed my chicks tonight," or some such remark, usually is excuse enough. Everyone smiles graciously at the figure and so the visit ends pleasantly. Whenever there seems to be no way to avoid being invited out on Sundays for dinner, make a grace out of a necessity.

III

TARGET PRACTICE

"For her my tears shall fall,
For her my prayers ascend;
To her my cares and toils be given,
Till toils and cares shall end."
—*Rev. Timothy Dwight.*

POSTPONE all analysis of your first Sunday's activities until you have been refreshed by sleep. Alexander Woollcott quotes Somerset Maugham as having said, that he always delivers an address four times. Once in the mind: "What I wish to say"; once on my feet: "What I did say"; once in the press: "What they report me as saying"; and once at midnight: "What I wish I had said." The idea is not a new one.

It is that midnight part which is so dangerous to preachers. Defer all judgment on the sermon until Monday morning when you may rise at six, slip from your bed, throw on a bath robe and slippers, sit by the window in your easy chair, and hold a post mortem; only then, and not before then, can you think clearly. It's a Monday morning reflection.

On one of these mornings one may take the Bible from a taboret and read Matthew 16: and then Ephesians 5. These pages give the direction to your thought "What kind of a church shall my church be?"

All the answers had been given in the Seminary: "The Church is a *body* whose head is Christ. It is a *bride*. Its character must be stainless. Its function is the mothering of God's Children. It is a *fellowship* of believers. It is a divine *organization*. 'I will build my church.' It is to be divinely *preserved*. 'The gates of hell shall not prevail.' It is a *government* whose constitution is the Bible. It has officers, ordinances, orders."

"My own denomination, a great body, rapidly growing, with a great history and great principles."

Come back in your thinking to the local congregation. Of far more importance is it, than all definitions or theories, to watch the attendance. The attendance should be kept carefully posted on a framed chart by the door; and on the same line, the text, the speaker, and the weather. A well executed graph will show the yearly fluctuation both morning and evening.

HOW TO GAUGE ONE'S OWN WORK

Compute the efficiency of the Church.

CHART I—ATTENDANCE

	A.M.	P.M.	
January	362	222	
February	376	230	
March	485	287	
April	426	201	Easter
May	482	187	
June	320	168	
July	247	115	
August	243	74	Vacation
September	337	157	
October	381	178	
November	288	133	An epidemic visited the city

December 317   507
AVERAGE 355   205

Membership 1001.
Per cent of efficiency, morning 36%.
Per cent of efficiency, evening 20%.

CHART II—ATTENDANCE AT THE LORD'S SUPPER

Present every Communion Sunday for twelve months, 12 persons.

Eleven months, 28

Ten months, 76

Nine months, 38

Eight months, 35

Seven months, 48

These 237 may be recorded in a book as regular communicants.

Six months, 47

Five months, 43

Four months, 50

These 140 mark with the letter "O" meaning that they come occasionally.

Three months, 46

Two months, 72

One month, 100

These 218 marked "seldom"

There are 219 more who never come. Some of these have acceptable reasons; the shut-in, the non-resident, and those attending the mission school, and many of these have asked to be excused. The church must provide a time and place when such as these may receive the emblems of the Lord's Table. There remain 187 names of those who never come and who never send a valid excuse. Most of these are on the non-resident or inactive roll. This situation and these names are the problem of the Official Church Body.

CHART III—CONTRIBUTORS

148 persons in 62 families pledge
335 pledge as individuals
47 non-residents send pledges
—
Total 530

But here are 471 who have no pledge at all. This list should be presented to the Trustees, the Finance Committee and the Collectors.

In some instances the officials do not think it wise for the Pastor to see the pledges. If so, assign the task to a layman. But get it done. Here are the final results of that survey:

5 paid $1820
17 paid 1821
31 paid 1612
77 paid 2153
267 paid 2103
47 paid 675 (non-residents)

Here were 444 pledges from 530 individuals and from these the church had realized $10,184.

Let them omit the names, if they insist, but ask to see the amounts recorded on the *last special subscription*. This special subscription has amounted let us say to $4,000 and this has come from 16% of the membership as follows:—

```
        20 gave $2000
        34 gave   790
       107 gave   965
       ───       ────
       161      $3755
    Sunday School
     Classes gave  245
                  ────
         Total $4000
```

By this time one is a poor guesser who does not know the names of the twenty folk needing pastoral care, possessing the greatest means.

CHART IV—THE BUDGET

Salaries $6,000
Music 1,000
Light and Fuel 1,000
Printing, stationery and Advertising.. 800
Interest, Insurance, Paving Repairs and
    Incidentals 1,200
                              ────$10,000
Benevolences 5,000
The benevolences were divided:—
City $1,400
State 1,000
Nation 900
World 1,300
Minister's pensions and education.... 400

This problem must be met by Christian vision and a long educative process. If some former pastor has been sufficiently methodical to leave records from which these rewarding surveys may be made, his records will prove of help. If that is not the case, then start to construct these statistical tables for the future, now.

If the attendance of the day before was well above four hundred, smile and wave your hand and say "New broom." Be the first to think of it.

Pull out a note book and write in fine script, "Remember to ask head usher if the weekly count is absolutely accurate." Call to mind the times when church attendance figures have seemed padded.

SIZE OF MEMBERSHIP

Resolve now that your church must never be larger than you can personally direct and supervise. Make a resolution, "I can and by God's help I will increase the membership by fifty per cent in seven years." The purpose of that is to give one's inert nature a challenging goal. Its danger lies in the tendency to become unfair and to steal sheep from adjoining pastures, or to let down the spiritual standards that govern all membership.

Arnold of Rugby said: "This is not bound to be a large school, young men, but it must be a school of gentlemen." One's best slogan is "My church shall be a spiritually minded church. If I can, I will make it a large church too."

An increasing number of our pastors of big congregations agree, that if the membership exceeds 2,000 one should urge the hive to swarm and to establish another branch or mission at least a mile from the home base. For reasons chiefly of fellowship and organization this seems to be a necessity.

THE CHURCH BUILDING

Early in every pastorate the edifice must be examined. It should be a good building. The Sanctuary must have good acoustic properties, and comfortable seats. It will be an advantage if there is a commodious vestry for the mid-week meetings and for all sorts of activities. There must be classrooms but these will never be enough; for the older organized classes always with short-sightedness take over these classrooms as their own. This is a prevalent sin and a colossal stupidity. There should be a nicely furnished ladies parlor, and a well equipped kitchen, a study, and a large vestibule. Has the building a debt? Professor Charles Richmond Henderson used to say that a building debt of more than $5.00 per resident member is too large. If one finds a large debt, he should write the Church Edifice Department of the Home Missionary Society about a conference on the matter. The location of the building is important, yet there is not much that can be done about a church's location. One cannot encourage the policy that abandons a building and builds expensive edifices at the Needle's Eye gate simply because the neighborhood is changing or deteriorating. One's congregation must be faced with the law of obligation. Thank God if you have a constituency widely distributed socially, for rich and poor, wise and unlearned, for the foreigner, Lithuanian, Armenian, Italian, German, French, Scandinavian. Yonder is a colored family in the balcony. Thank God, again. Like Booker T. Washington we do not want the races of another color for our brothers-in-law, but we do want them for our brothers.

The problem of race prejudice lies deep. The French do not like the Irish. The Arab does not like his cousin, the Jew.

The Japanese Islanders fight the more ancient ancestral line on the mainland, the Chinese and Koreans. Put a group of Jews together in one room. To you, they are all Jews. Not so, to them. The German, despises the Polish Jew. Both despise the Portuguese, worst of all.

We are not fifty years removed from bitter controversy along racial lines. Small wonder that negroes and whites meet with occasional difficulty. But let us not intensify something in our own nature that is as old as the first dog fight, just outside the garden of Eden.

"God . . . hath made of one blood all nations of men."

"We are pioneers and in the morn of destiny," Tennyson reminds us. There are many lessons to learn; one of these is the way white folks and black folks and brown folks and yellow folks can live together. We Christians may be able to point the way.

FREE SEATS

If the seats are free, the church has removed one great problem; that, of social differences, and cleavages and cliques and awareness of pride and prejudice. But it may bring a similar problem if the people become so attached to one pew, that to all intents, they own it.

DENOMINATIONAL EFFICIENCY REPORT

Read the report of the committee on church efficiency of one of the denominational groups:

"Believing that we, as a denomination, should set before ourselves and persistently undertake to realize higher ideals of life and service than those that now appear in our church life, we therefore most earnestly recommend that the churches shall hold before themselves the following standard of efficiency:

(1) Every member should render some form of personal *service* in the varied ministry of the church.

(2) Every member should *give* proportionately—according to ability and need—to the local expenses of the church and to the spread of the gospel throughout the world.

(3) Every member, as a learner in the *school* of Christ, should teach or be taught in the educational work of the church.

(4) Every church should have a constructive program for serving the *social needs* of its community, either individually or through the largest possible co-operation with other organizations for human uplift.

(5) Wherever possible the local church should co-operate with other local bodies for increased fellowship and efficiency.

(6) *Non-resident* membership should be reduced to the minimum."

The report says much; but not enough. In the light of it you as a pastor must ask yourself; "But what shall be my aim?" Set down upon paper the five things one will consciously try to attain, without attempting to set one thing as more important than another.

SET UP YOUR OWN TARGET

(1) I will try to make my church an educational institution. A woman's magazine carries the story of a poor West Virginian living back in the hills who discovers oil, coal and gas on his land. Suddenly he finds himself possessed of great riches. In order to settle his income tax, he sends for a judge from the city. The judge drives from the station through the mud and finds the dreary log cabin, the unkempt wife, and

the slatternly daughters. Chickens chase across the kitchen floor, and pigs root in the front dooryard.

"What do you think of the way we live?" the man asks of the judge repeatedly. Unable longer to evade the question, the judge replies, "I think you live like swine."

"So do I," said the man. "What can we do about it?"

"Subscribe for The Farm and Fashion Magazine!" was the advice.

A year later the judge returned to find a transformation—a fine bungalow, landscape gardening, a fine car, trained servants, wife and daughters becomingly clad, the table spread with snowy linen and expensive silver.

"How did you do it?" asked the judge.

"I subscribed for Farm and Fashion," was the reply.

How are we to take our untrained worldling newly won to Christ and furnish his mind in such a way as to make him the obedient servant of heaven?

I must educate, is at least one answer. I must acquaint my people with the Bible, and Church history, and get them to subscribe to a church paper, with the promise, if possible, that they will aim to read it each week.

(2) I will aim to make my church a worshipping church. President William Rainey Harper of the University of Chicago, said less than a year before his death, in speaking of the Old Testament, "No one knows a book by having another read it for him." So it is with worship.

Encourage private acts of piety; Bible reading and personal prayer. Do all in your power to promote public worship. One day the telephone bell rang, and a voice commanded: "Come over at once to Blue's Mortuary for a service."

I was met at the door by an assistant who said, "You have

only twenty minutes for this service." I looked inside the door and saw a casket in a vacant room.

"Where are the mourners?"

"There are none," came the reply.

"What do you expect me to do?"

"Why ask me. Here is the record card. We are shipping the remains back to his home. We are instructed by wire to hold a Christian service. Go in and perform your office."

My first feeling was that it would be a sacrilege or a meaningless form to offer a prayer as if it were a service of public worship if none were present, not even two or three, to hear. Then it swept over me with the speed of light that such a situation should present no problem. I was not performing a service for man, or to man but in the Unseen Presence. I would put the seal of worth upon a human life and do it with none but God to hear. I recited a psalm, offered a prayer and made a commital before I withdrew.

The recognition of God is the essence of worship. A worshipping soul deals with God and is or should be competent in spite of numbers. "Fear not little flock it is the Father's good pleasure to give you the Kingdom." "For where two or three are gathered together in my name there am I in the midst of them." The essence of worship is God and a surrendered soul, in communion.

(3) I will aim to develop giving in my church into a grace.

A friend of mine tells me that when he was a child, working over the looms in Scotland, he brought to his mother his first pay envelope. "There, mither, is my pay." It was about the equivalent of a dollar and a half.

"Is it a' yours?"

"Aye, it's a' mines, mither!"

"Na, Na, the tithe belongs to Goad. Ye'll pie it at the Kirk, the morn."

"Pay God ten cents out of every dollar you earn." At first I obeyed her. Then there came a day when I no longer *paid* it. I *gave* it instead, passing so, out of the Old Testament into the New. The tithe does present difficulties. For the poor man it seems too much. For the man of large means it seems too little. But from time to time speak of it, suggesting also, regular proportionate giving. Begin a clipping file on the subject of giving and for the first story file the following:—

The Jewish Synagog at Dantzic many years ago decided to make its rabbi a gift to celebrate his fiftieth anniversary as head of the community, according to a story that might have started with Heinrich Heine. As the rabbi was growing old and infirm it was decided to give him a hogshead of wine to cheer, refresh and strengthen him. It was agreed that the head of each family should appear at the rabbi's house on the jubilee day and bring a bottle of good Rhine wine. The rabbi naturally wished to entertain his guests, and he therefore offered all of them a glass of wine. Imagine his and their astonishment when it was found that the barrel contained nothing but water. Each and every one of the givers thinking that one bottle of water in a whole barrel of wine would not be detected and therefore would make no practical difference in its taste, had filled his bottle with water.

Human nature is pretty much the same, the world over. The Dantzic story is unmistakably apocryphal, and it bears the ear marks of a racial joke. But salvation is still altogether too free.

(4) I will aim to give my church a passion for the social ills of the community and the world.

"Come to the county jail," comes another voice over the telephone.

Take along your wealthiest woman. The bailiff leads you down a corridor to the cell block. The girl is evidently a Hungarian. There has been a strike in the box factory. Taught "the ropes" by her roommate she has taken to the street, the easy way. Here is her story: "At first there was a little fun in it. But the cops got me. And now I guess I'm done for." She sobs piteously. Then the realization may dawn upon you that any environment that damns a human life must be changed in the name of Christ. The Cross becomes a demand that we die to make things right. War, racialism and economic inequality are but a beginning of the wrongs there are in society. And the Christian does have a social obligation, not merely to regret or to deplore these conditions, but to do something definite to bring about a proper solution.

I recall an experience with one of my professors, when at Columbia. It meant little then. The professor had conducted a course in Ethics. The examination was held in the professor's home.

We were seated about the room on chairs and even on the floor rugs. A fire burned cheerily in the grate. In the group sat the doctor's little daughter. There was a Jew and a Catholic and a Mohammedan in the class and more than a dozen others. After the blank paper was passed out he said, "Young men, I shall ask you only one question, tonight. What will be the first question God will ask you after you are dead?"

There was a singular similarity in the answers; "Have you been good?"

The answers were read aloud and then the leader quietly said, "I don't think that will be the question."

His little daughter sharing in the tension of the moment bubbled, "Oh, papa, you're only fooling."

Disregarding the interruption he went on. "Most of us believe in a God whose very name is Sacrifice. We live in an expanding universe. All the rays of light and heat and love and life always flow outward. That's the meaning of the Cross. Jesus lived on earth and found things wrong. He could not go away and leave it until he righted the wrong even unto his death. I imagine then that God might say to you, 'Where did you live? Did you find everything all right there? Did you try hard to set things right?'"

In the light of that experience of student days, I seem to hear Jesus saying, "If any man would come after me let him deny himself."

The cross topples over on us but we hear its victim saying, "You will help me change the world."

So far we have constructed a good program but it lacks something. Education, worship, generosity, social passion. What is left out?

(5) Evangelism. Read Ephesians 4:11-12. The plain implication of Paul here seems to be that no pastor has fulfilled his function who has not perfected the saints of his congregation in the work of the ministry. He trains them to be evangelists. Thus he multiplies his voice of invitation.

A friend of mine gives me this personal experience. He assures me of its truth. He had been terribly ill. It seemed as if his ministerial usefulness was fast slipping from him. He seemed to dream. Perhaps it was the drug that had been administered. When he awoke he rose, went to his wife's desk and wrote it down as he gave it to me and I give it to you. The sickness had left him. The veil was gone from his mind. He has been an effective servant of God for a score of years since. This is his story:

"I dreamed that I died. I struggled for a moment as a small boy might struggle to get out of his clothes for bed. Presently I was in the upper air, walking through a lovely field of shaded blue, varying from the light of a baby's eyes to the deepest ultra-marine. And through the field was a path of gold. At the end of the path was a city as lovely as a cumulus cloud. And from the city came music.

"I kept meeting groups of angels, clad in flowing Grecian draperies, and in each instance they were laughing and talking happily but not boisterously. They were in groups of two and three and all going in an opposite direction. 'Hello, little brother!' they said.

"At last I met a slightly larger group, and I sensed that the leader was my angel. But I did not understand what it could mean.

"They waited for me to speak. I said, 'I'm going to heaven; is God at home?'

" 'No,' said my angel, 'He's almost never there.'

"I wondered if they were playing on me some monstrous post-mortem joke. I said, 'Where is he, then?'

"And the leader replied, 'He's in the hell you came from.'

"Then I thought my angel took me almost roughly and said, 'He's down there on Calvary. He's doing the job you ran away from.'

"He paused a moment and said to me: 'Little brother, when you were on the earth did you never hear Christ saying, "He that seeketh to save his life shall lose it." '

" 'Little brother, that place would not be heaven for you yonder. It is but the hell of selfish men who have gone there alone, thinking of heaven as a way of escape. Escape? Escape is only a first step. One may escape from habit. One may escape from evil desire. But one escapes only to set others free.'

" 'Look!' He took me by the shoulders and turned me round. I saw below me a yawning depth. Blood and fire and vapor of smoke and dimly, I saw a cross.

"With bated breath, almost in a whisper, I said 'What is that?'

" 'The suffering world from which you came.'

"And I put my hand in his, and we swung out over the great abyss, to come back to my ministry again. I knew that God was near for in my heart I felt a great yearning."

KEEP THE PROGRAM BEFORE YOU

Why not have these five things typed and framed and hung above the desk in your Church study or inserted in your appointment book where you will be constantly reminded of it:

My Program	It Will Require
1. Educate	1. Thought
2. Worship	2. Time
3. Give	3. Treasure
4. Serve	4. Talent
5. Save	5. Toil

There may then come a day when your work with this congregation is done. How shall one know? How can you evaluate your work?

Five standards will help you decide:

(1) The relative numbers who attend.

(2) The numbers who are being received into fellowship.

(3) The prompt payment of all obligations.

(4) The general air of peace and good will in the membership.

(5) Does one still have the confidence of the leading officials of his church?

IV

REMEMBERING NAMES AND FACES

A parish priest of austerity,
Climbed up in a high church steeple,
To be nearer God, that he might hand
His word down to the people.

And in sermon script, he daily wrote
What he thought was sent from heaven,
And dropped it down on the people's heads,
Two times, one day in seven.

In his age, God said, come down and die;
And he cried, from out the steeple,
"Where art thou Lord?" and the Lord replied,
"Down here among my people."
—Author unknown.

THE new pastor and his wife will be voted into the fellowship of the church in regular fashion like any other member. They will be given the Right Hand of Christian Fellowship at the first service in commemoration of the Lord's Supper by the officer duly designated to do this for the congregation.

Before the end of the month one has rented a house in the section of town where most of his people live. He has installed a telephone; furnished the house modestly; put in the winter's coal; had the house connected for water, gas and electricity; visited the post office and given most careful directions about mail; conferred with his church treasurer, and arranged for banking; and has chosen a grocer and market.

The church itself may finance for him an inexpensive but well-built automobile, which thereafter he cares for himself. If they are unable to do this perhaps a person with a car and some spare time will give much aid in the pastoral calling. Many such will give a day a week.

PASTOR'S RECEPTION

The President of the Woman's Society and the pastor's wife probably before the end of the week, will agree upon a time for the Pastor's Reception. It should be approximately one month from the date of his coming. It entails much labor. The committee on invitations sends word to all other pastors in the community, inviting them and their people. The invitations if marked should read "Informal." The committee on the program provides an orchestra perhaps, with suitable decorations and light refreshments, and asks the President of the Minister's Association to bring brief felicitations. The Pastor responds.

The young men of the Baraca Class in tuxedoes, if desired, and the young women of the Quests in formal gowns may usher. The receiving line will consist of the moderator of the congregation and his wife, the President of the Woman's Society and her husband and the pastor's entire family. The Chairman of the Board of Ushers will stand near to see that the line does not loiter.

The church officials should be in the line of those first received and then the visiting clergy. One senses from the start that here is a battle of wits. He will meet practically the entire parish and many from other churches. He and his wife must, therefore, both come to the ordeal with rested bodies. He realizes that if he is to remember names he must listen and attend. His mind is to be alert. The first hundred are easy. They compose the group one has already met at the station, with whom one has corresponded, and those who were present at the first prayer service. Here are his ushers, his choir, his Sunday School teachers. The exercises of welcome while not prolonged are sufficiently long so that one may look about appraisingly. If one looks at the group *en masse* he knows no one.

ONE MUST REMEMBER

But if one looks more scrutinizingly he realizes that he knows many. If some head looms above the crowd he does not hesitate to say to the Moderator, "Who is that?" Often his judgment will be justified. "Oh, yes! I'm glad you asked. That's Mr. and Mrs. Jones. She has a million. They're just home from California. They missed being present at your coming."

To this matter of attention one adds the function of personal interest, and links with them association of ideas. After the first three hundred one's mind will hold no more, except an occasional name, seen on the roll. But elimination helps. Make scant effort to remember the outsiders. That can come later. But one's own! There flagging attention quickens.

The credit man at B. Altman and Company in New York City makes himself remember three thousand customers' accounts. Why not try a proven method? Here's how it works: attention, personal interest, and association.

Identical twins come by. One is married. "I shall not remember you," you think. Oh, yes you will. The married one is speaking. She lifts herself on tip toe and whispers, "I'm the pretty one." He looks. And surely enough she is. One should not easily forget her.

Young business men identical twins are in the line. The only discernible difference is in the part of the hair. *David divides* his in the center. *Ernest* parts his on the *edge*. Here is an association which memory will store.

Next comes a lovely matron with gray hair. She waits for recognition, but it does not come. With seeming petulance she says, "If you can't do better than that, I'm not coming again." Then you recall the woman in smock with disheveled coiffure whom you had seen in the shadows, decorating, in the afternoon. After this your memory of personality must be divorced from dress. And you *must* remember.

Two sisters come by, Sarah and Tabitha Holyoke. One tall, the other short. How will you remember these. You ask their names again. That is it. Don't hurry. Take time. Make the ushers pronounce the names plainly. Ask for the spelling even. People like to be the center of interest. Sarah! Oh! Now you see that she is short. And Tabitha is tall. S, for short. T, for tall. That helps you.

Here is a little outlander, his face very pale. "My name is Litt." What is there here to remember? The pastor holds the hand a moment and smiles. Mr. Litt smiles in return and a most gorgeous piece of golden dentistry lights up his face. Rememberable now forever!

And here come another pair of twins, Junius beside his taller brother Augustus. He reflects a moment. Of course, June is one day shorter than August. Always the law of association helps one to remember.

Although one is very tired, before one sleeps one ought to go back over the events of the evening and make the mind recall as many individuals as possible, and pronounce their names aloud.

By the following week a group of helpers will have the entire church list arranged by districts, streets or offices. Then one must start seriously on his first complete visitation. By a definite time one has visited every home in the entire membership.

On Sundays one may announce on what streets one will be on a given day. One comes to know in this way the problems men are facing, physical, mental, social, financial, spiritual. One makes a notation of anniversaries as he travels, births, deaths, weddings. In the office he transfers this information to a card catalogue for each day of the year.

July 9th

Harvey Jones	1881 Born
John Sycamore	1899 Married
Mrs. Ambruster's	Husband died 1918

On one of these cards may be listed also dates of official importance to the church, such as its founding, its annual meeting, the date of the state, district and national meetings and the dates of the summer conferences.

In another file one will keep a card for every prospective new member. If Mrs. John Johnson's husband is not a member, make a note of it as you call. By the end of December one will have a prospect list of many names. The time to make a record of data is when one receives it. The best minds forget. No mind can carry all the information one receives on the first calling tour. It will be needed later; and as long as this particular pastorate continues, it will be of great value. Keep it. And keep it *sacred*.

Six weeks before Easter cards may be placed in the pews for an enrollment of those attending. On the back of the card make an opportunity to record certain items.

(1) Please sing my favorite hymn No. .....
(2) Please preach from my favorite chapter .....
(3) I volunteer for the following service .....
(4) I am interested in church membership.

The back of the card will intrigue the interest of the congregation. The front of the card will intrigue the Pastor. Every Tuesday morning, sort these cards to determine who of the membership are attending, who are lukewarm, and who are thinking seriously of uniting with the church.

BROADENING FRIENDSHIPS

Consult the Public Library for the history of the community and prepare an address on "My City's Tomorrow," from the text "Tomorrow shall be as this day, and much more abundant." Isa. 56:12. Ask the Chamber of Commerce and the service clubs to attend in a body, on a Sunday evening.

One may be able by careful study to make a daring prophecy that the population will increase rapidly. One must be sure of one's facts on which to base a prediction. Or one may foresee a slump and suggest ways to avert it. The ice is thin here but it can be done, helpfully. This service will widen the acquaintance of a pastor with his city and its leaders.

When one has demonstrated that he really can do such a thing, he may visit the principal of the High School and possibly may be invited to speak at Assembly. If this comes one must prepare what he has to say with the utmost care, remembering that youth forgives anything but length and dullness. The Platte River in Nebraska is a constant admonition. It is a mile wide and a foot deep: long, shallow, muddy. One has heard addresses like that.

Acquaintance with the schools greatly helps one. "He's a good sport. Dad, you should have heard him. And he knew when to stop. He had a lovely smile. And gee! he knows a lot. He's even been to New York City or some place." But one must exercise care lest he take on too much and spread himself thin.

Few pastors have the time to be good lodge men. But if a member, attend on the night of inspection, and pass all tests favorably. On the anniversary day of the founder one may invite an organization to attend his church in a body. But remember that other pastors will covet this honor, too. One needs to be reminded that one does not enlarge his congregation permanently by such anniversary services. If you're looking for permanent growth, cultivate the more fruitful ground elsewhere.

One may easily become a slave, caught in a mechanistic labyrinth from which there is no escape. When Mark Mathews comes into a gathering he makes it his custom to say, "Brethren, you are having a meeting today, which I wanted to attend. I cannot stay long, however; I have an appointment (naming the hour). But the brief moment I spend here will be a blessing to me and I hope it will be to you. When it is necessary for me to go, I will slip out." And so he keeps his contacts but yet keeps himself free.

You will be interested to know that the man with a church of nine thousand members, the largest white church in America, does it. I have gone with him in an evening when we made contact with nine different meetings.

With diligence, by the end of the year one knows every face, and name, of both young and old of both sexes in his congregation and in addition knows many of his townspeople, of all classes and groups. When he passes down the street he moves among these, feeling: "I know my sheep."

PASTORAL VISITATION

Every week he visits the hospital. But he visits the Superintendent first or the person in charge of the desk. He ascertains carefully where a pastoral call would be welcomed. He learns the art of getting into a sick room without noise and getting out just quickly enough, and with a smile that is itself a prayer. He tells the call desk unostentatiously that he is available at any hour of day or night for any type of case whatsoever.

He keeps his calls carefully tabulated in a calling book with date and hour of call. This may prove important. If one is calling on the neurotic, he does not call alone. He takes a trusted person with him.

When he begins his own pastoral visitation he makes his first care the aged and the sick. Next he visits the disinterested and disaffected. Later he begins the systematic visitation. But he keeps one half day early in the week in which to visit cases of birth or extreme illness, or emergency. If a person shows an interest in church membership, these too come under the emergency class. Not later than Friday of every week he and his wife check carefully to see that no socially obligatory call has been neglected.

His work will not have progressed far before he realizes that while he is doing much it must be supplemented by many hands of friendship. These helpers must be chosen carefully for they must truly represent the Church and its spirit of love.

His women will undertake an old-fashioned church sociable, not a dinner nor a play, nor a revenue producing affair at all, but a meeting for the merging and cementing of interest.

A little later he will ask for a Planning Council to be at a supper attended by all the officers of every department.

After the first fifty new members have come into the fellowship under his leadership he will arrange a New Members Supper for them when several speakers stress anew the meaning of church finance, the prayer meeting, worship, youth's place, literature, and woman's work; and the meeting will end with a suitable response from one of the more capable of the novices.

At the minister's meeting if he can do it without seeming an upstart, he may propose an exchange on the Sunday following immediately after Easter, in which each man puts his hand in the hat and goes to the other field he draws.

When the evening service is functioning successfully he may announce at its close a fellowship service in the vestry, where a few of the more devout will gather for a song and closing prayer. It gives the opportunity to speak an intimate word about Christ to some who are deeply moved. This service may be continued each year until about Easter. It will cement the social and religious interest and many will be won in such a service that would not have come otherwise.

The Catholic Church has done this for centuries, calling it Compline or Even Song, the last service of the day. One marvels at their canny psychology that knows all angles of the heart.

VISITORS WHO ASSIST

After one has completed the pastoral visitation, he supplies his officials with selected lists of members and after they have voted to receive these he gives each official the following letter: (This letter has been chosen because it proved exceptionally effective.)

Dear Friend and Helper:

In giving you this list, I give you a difficult task. For one year you are to be the pastor of these people whose cards you have. You are to learn their names, addresses, natures, problems. If they are lost you are to find them. You are to pray over them in your heart as if their salvation depended on you. You are to report changes of address to the church office. Can God trust you to know all about them, yet never, under any circumstances, to reveal to outsiders their problems?

Some on your list are the best saints on earth; some of them are a problem, even to themselves. Are you wise enough to know these facts, and make allowances? Have you disciplined your own heart so that you will hear their complaints and judge them in the light of eternity? In making pastoral calls, one sometimes meets difficult people. You may. Can you be sweet tempered, tactful and silent? These are what will test whether you have any business to be in charge of this list. Church officers are called of God to the task as much as have been pastors. In the old days, pastors were usually chosen from persons who were Deacons first. Exhaust every resource of your own in trying to get these folks faithful to Christ and the Church before you come to the

Pastor for aid. That's why you are being asked to do it. To lighten the burden all around.

Report to the office promptly all important information, especially serious illness, deaths, births. Get busy at once. Time has a way of going by rapidly. Some of you will let a month go by, if you are not careful, before you make the first call. Do not say to any of the list that you are their overseer. That would spoil everything. Let them think what they may. But let them feel a genuine, not an official, interest. Please bear in mind that your duty is not done until you have given personal attention to every person. Do not think that one call at an address is enough. Look up individuals away from home at the time you call.

You will make mistakes perhaps. Most people do. But we learn by doing. There is joy in action. As you try to do this work faithfully, may you have the happiest year you have ever known.

You will find some of the people on your list at places of business. In every call you make, please have your mind attentive to possible prospects for membership.

Anyone can fail. It takes a good person to succeed. Let's set for ourselves the high standard of not accepting, even from ourselves, any excuse for failure. I have invited a few people like you who are not church officials to assist. Thank you.

Affectionately your pastor,

This letter accompanies a printed or mimeographed folder, on the front page of which appears the title, "In Your Keeping," and the name and address of the local church; on the back page is given the complete list of the deacons and deaconesses who are engaged in this monthly check.

Here on the following page is a condensed reproduction of the inside of this folder. The full names and addresses of the church membership allotted to each deacon or deaconess are given on his folder. Note that on the folder ample space is given for marking the *type* of check-up. (See key at the upper right-hand corner of the card.)

OUR AIM. Contact each Church member once a month by one of the following methods. Contact at a Church service, telephone or mail.

Mark card with following legend: A.M. Attended morning service. P.M. Attended evening service. F. Friday service. C. Called. T. Telephoned. M. Mail. N.C. No Contact. A.C.F. Attempted contact failed.

NAME	ADDRESS	TEL.	CKPL*	JUNE	JULY	AUG.	SEPT.	OCT.	NOV.	DEC.	JAN.	FEB.	MAR.	APR.	MAY

* check pledge.

V

JEWISH NEIGHBORS

Shall Jew and Gentile meeting
From many a distant shore,
Around one altar kneeling
One common Lord adore?
    —*Jane Bosthwick, 1859.*

ON ORCAS ISLAND, one of the large islands in the San Juan
group, on our northwest boundary there is a herd of deer, none
of them larger than a good sized dog. Their story is the story
of inbreeding. A buck and doe on the mainland sometime
prior to 1845, pursued by hunters, took to the sea and caught
by tide rips were carried to this hospitable shore. They bred
and their progeny survive, a constant reminder that the blood
stream of any organism needs replenishment.

If one doubts this problem of the human race, let him visit
those large families of twenty or more, dwelling in the sheltered valleys of the Appalachian Range of Eastern Kentucky
and Tennessee.

Immigration presents its own set of problems, chiefly economic, partly neighborly and religious; but biologically, it has
been a blessing. As one crosses our continent he is led to observe the nature of this infiltration. To begin at my door,
Somerville, Massachusetts is almost entirely peopled from the
maritime provinces. One good naturedly speaks of the "Blue-
nose" Nova Scotian; or the "Herring-Choker," from New
Brunswick.

An examination of the records of my own city of Lowell at the Chamber of Commerce reveals the following:

Population 100,234.

Total white foreign born or mixed parentage, 46,994.

England	4209	Lithuania	317
Scotland	1169	Latvia	28
Wales	58	Finland	28
N. Ireland	1813	Rumania	16
Irish Free State	11,461	Greece	2542
Norway	114	Italy	519
Sweden	478	Portugal	1189
Denmark	26	Armenia	210
Netherlands	23	Palestine	330
Belgium	34	Turkey	122
Switzerland	5	Canada (French)	14,417
France	106	Canada (all other)	3,429
Poland	2580	Newfoundland	215
Czecho Slovakia	16	Azores	74
Austria	62	All other	613
Russia	791		

The 3000 Jews in the above record are not listed by religion but are recorded by the country from which they came. There is no listing of Negroes, nor Catholics, nor Protestants, nor Greek Orthodox as such. Yet one becomes aware of these, and of the native born whose family goes back to the early days of the American Colonies.

While my congregation is homogeneously American, I find almost a score of national, racial and creedal groups, as the springs that feed into our stream of church life. If one drives across Rhode Island, he becomes aware of the Portuguese who have intermarried with the Narragansett Indians. In Lawrence, Massachusetts he sees Mona Lisa stepping out of her frame and walking down the street. The story of the immigrant in

America is so familiar to us that it scarcely needs notice, no matter where we live.

The South side of Chicago is dominantly Negro. "North Carolina and Florida are no longer Southern, but northern states in population," remarked a friend in Atlanta.

The Welsh coal miner has come to Scranton. A fine German stock has planted Dunkard, (German-Baptist) communities throughout Indiana.

In the Twin Cities one expects his congregation to be one-third German, one-third Scandinavian, and one-third old American racial stock. In Seattle, one finds the South. In Los Angeles, is New England and much else, including the Mexican.

In upper Michigan, the copper mines could not be operated without the Cornishman.

EVERY CONGREGATION IS FOREIGN

A strong bodied, blue-eyed man with intelligent face passes out the church door.

"Comment t'allez vous, monsieur?" or in the idiom "Comment ce va?"

"Tres bien, merci, et vous?"

You are met with a rewarding smile. Or it may be a Slovak! "I want to see your drawings." You may be sure he is an artist, of talent.

A Welshman. "Bendegeddig! Goganiant." "Praise the Lord, Hallelujah."

A Scandinavian. "Jag är glad, du är här!"

He looks at you quickly and responds with a smile, "Tak sa mikit."

One member of a race should not lead us to generalizations. Because one man is a "square head," heavy with "snoose" and "booze" it does not follow that his race is sodden nor that they are dull.

A timid little Japanese, pigeontoes by. You say in low voice, "Ohayo Gozaimasu?" "How do you do, honored sir?" Do not omit the "mas." It is the badge of dignity. You have pleased him for an entire day.

The next man may be a Pole. "Jak sie masz?" (pron: Yak shemash.)

He replies "Dobrze." (Dobe zha) (All right).

My Scot friend has been watching. He is next in line. "Hoo are ye, the morn, mon?"

"Brawley, mon, thank ye for spierin'."

Even the Greek is here. "Kal' heméra." Your new testament Greek comes to your aid.

"A lovely day, indeed, sir."

And so they continue to come by. As the tides of all oceans wash our shores in response to the call of the moon, so the tidal waves of human life from every land dash themselves upon the hard resisting rocks of misunderstanding in every state and city.

The sum total of your performance is not a demonstration that you are mentally alert; nor is it an encouragement to the immigrant to retain habits or customs which he should discard; but it is a friendly hand of good will. You have said, "I am sufficiently interested in you, to have mastered at least one phrase of your tongue so that you may feel at home." He will now come again.

The Armenians at first were so friendly. Then they became more reserved, after the assassination of their Arch-bishop.

Perhaps a mother's meeting could be arranged for them. For as long as they attend you will see the head of the child Jesus, nestling in your congregation.

Your Chinese school, on Sunday afternoon, will require one teacher for every scholar. If the teachers are women, they must be mature. Among the Orientals you cease to say, "They all look alike." You soon distinguish the fat, well-favored and educated Manchu restaurant proprietor, from the Cantonese laundryman. You distinguish both, from the spade faced Korean, or the smart Japanese. You learn never to say "Jap" and "Chinaman." Always, "Japanese" and "Chinese."

If a Philippine house boy sits in your prayer service and interrupts with, "You lie!" you remember first that they are emotionally quick and second that they are outspoken. He probably means no more than your more polite friend who says, "I beg your pardon."

You ask him to help you with your facts—which he is pleased to do.

When I came to New England, the former home of my parents, a place I had never visited, it was I for the first six months, who spoke an alien tongue. For a month I did not call a telephone number that the patient operator did not say, "Again, please."

My secretary smiled when I asked for the water cooler.

"The waw-terr is therr," she mocked me.

The Sunday night before, one of my youth had read I Cor. 13: What I seemed to hear was this. "Foh we know in pat and we prophesy in pat, but when that which is *pay'-eye-fickt* is come, then that which is in pat shall be done away."

Some time ago I was coming out of a restaurant after a modest lunch, and in the approach of the doorway I saw a man, coming towards me. There was something familiar about him, and I was debating in my mind where I had seen him before and how I should address him when we met, as was inevitable in the narrow passage. To my astonishment, just before we should have come face to face with each other, I discovered that I was walking toward a mirror, and the man I was to meet was myself! I never quite realized before, that I looked so. "Can that be I?" I said involuntarily. "What has suddenly happened to me?" It was a moment of realization. I saw myself full-length, as I am.

I confess that prejudice is not dead in my heart. To cure my own soul I observe Brotherhood Day the second Sunday of February. The priest will not come, unless permitted by the Archbishop. I invite a Catholic layman of prominence instead. The Jewish cantor gladly consents to sing for us "Rachem," "Have mercy." As he passes out the door we exchange greetings, "Shalom."

A friendship with the Rabbi that I have never ceased to thank God for, develops. He taught my men's class well. Later he spoke in the evening service and invited me to speak at his. He attends our ministers meeting regularly.

I had preached on the universal love of God to all men and had told my congregation that a part of the test of our Christianity is to be found in the way we rid our hearts of hate toward other peoples and creeds.

Now I was faced with an invitation to test my theories in the white hot crucible of actual experience. "Come over and tell my people honestly what Christians think of them."

I accepted, and went. I spoke on "The Christian's Debt to the Jew." I was asked to preach with my hat on, at the close of what seemed to me a very strange service performed for

the most part in Hebrew. I read as my text Romans 3:1 and
1:14, and added: "and Paul might have said 'I am a debtor to
the Jew.'" I spoke of my own denomination as also an ex
parte group which had often felt the sting of ridicule or the
fires of persecution, and then launched into my subject.

"The average Christian honestly entertains toward the
average Hebrew a four fold attitude. His first attitude is
one of admiration: *admiration for his financial ability*. They
are the bankers of the world. For while he may jest with
Shakespeare about Shylock he secretly admires his Rothschilds,
and Kuhns and Rosenwalds. *He admires the Jewish quality
of cohesiveness*. The Jews stand together. The more they
are persecuted the more compact they become. Persecution
has never mastered them in Egypt under Pharaoh, in Persia
under Haman, in Greece under Antiochus, in Russian po-
groms under the Czars, nor in the ghettos of Central Europe.
The Jew is more cohesive than a postage stamp; more united
than a mob in an alley fight. It is part of the tradition of
Protestants that we are individualists. If two meet, we agree
only upon what a third party shall give to the Community
Chest.

"Not so, the Jew. *We admire their racial solidarity*. They
have gone into every nation. They do not intermarry; or if
they do they are what the Eugenicist would call dominant.
You can no more conquer them than you can the Chinese.
There are not over 15,000,000 of them in the world yet their
influence is as strong as a great Christian organization, not
Protestant, over twenty times as large. We admire this soul
force.

"*Our second attitude is one of apology*. Not pity. We do
pity their suffering. Yet no one but a child wishes for pity.

Our attitude is deeper. We are apologetic for the persecution and the derision, heaped upon them by Christian nations.

" 'Poor Sheeny Levy,' will hardly square with the Golden Rule of which we so loudly boast. It seems almost an irony of fate that a Gentile outside the law, wishing to convert a Jew, should by his very attachment to a crucified Savior come to hate the Jew. Jews dread the return of our greatest holiday lest by our most sacred emblems we stir anew a fresh hatred.

"I myself was present at a theatre mass meeting of Christians in a building owned and operated by a Jew and loaned by his courtesy and heard the speaker give a speech proving that it was the Jew who crucified Jesus; but although those Jews have been dead for nearly two thousand years, his speech became more and more inflammatory and vitriolic as it neared its close, toward the children of those distant peoples. How can we reconcile such conduct with the Jesus who died saying, 'Father, forgive.'

"*Our attitude is also one of concern.* Many Christians pray for their Jewish brethren as earnestly as for any people on earth. A part of the popularity of such a play as 'Abie's Irish Rose,' lay in its genuine concern to see the problem of separation between peoples and creeds solved.

"*The average Christian believes in the ultimate triumph of the Jew.* They do not understand many of the eddies and currents and ripples within Judaism itself, having to do with Zionism, but they believe that the Bible predicts that the Jew will come to his own land, and that he will come to a high exaltation. I do not expect you to agree with this, but I honestly think it.

"*Toward Judaism as a religion the Christian frankly recognizes a difference.* Christianity is not Judaism. Our day is different. Our customs are different. Our food, our initiatory rite, our Leader are all different. Many Christians fear formalism, and look with fear upon any system of legalism. Most Christians would hold here most tenaciously.

"But every well informed Christian also recognizes an attitude which we all take toward Judaism as a historic source. That attitude is one of indebtedness. We owe to Judaism what the branch owes to the trunk, what the child owes to the family line, what today owes to yesterday. From the Jew we have our faith in one God. Our possession of a preserved Bible; our moral law; our sabbath. Our Christian sabbath is our most prized possession. It is the center pillar to our temple. It is priceless, even though some may kick it about like the unlettered Boer did his diamond paper weight, thinking it only a stone. And we get this possession from the Jew.

"From Ezra we derive our technique of worship. Even the despised tithe provided us the clue to the free support of our free institutions.

"And greater than all the rest we get Jesus himself. Born a Jew. I concluded with these words: "We as Christians recognize that we cannot go backward any more than I can go back to my father's house. But I can be grateful for the rich inheritance the Jews have given me and I can hope to share the riches of that inheritance with them, whom I know to be God's Chosen People."

The impact of the sermon upon the entire community was wholesome. I had without stultification or evasion clearly stated an issue. I furnished the reporter at the service with an unexpurgated copy of my address, with which to insure accuracy. And this was released the following morning. I gained more by that service than any single service I ever held.

My name for freedom from bigotry went from group to group through the city. The Catholics respected me. The laboring man came to feel that a man who would state his case so frankly could be trusted in a pinch. Yet all I had done was to demonstrate Brotherhood without the sacrifice of a single conviction. Even yet, I don't see that I did anything more than try to answer one of my own prayers. "Brethren, my heart's desire and prayer to God for Israel is that they might be saved."

As the result of a similar service, held by another, one was baptized, a New Testament given to a second, while the son of a third entered the Christian Sunday School. Yet, I do not urge Christian conduct toward other peoples because it pays in church membership, but because it is right. If one can do it for the Jew, why not attempt it, for those of other races, nations or creeds.

VI

THE ORGANIZATIONAL SET-UP

"My Father worketh hitherto and I work."—*John 5:17*.

". . . The Head from which all the body by joints and bands having nourishment ministered and knit together, increaseth with the increase of God."—*Col. 2:19*.

THIS chapter concerns the organizational set-up of every church, its constitution, its by-laws, its committees, officers and boards, the frame work that holds it together.

A careful kindly non-critical appraisal of the average church causes a great leader like Dr. George Irving to believe five things concerning it:

1. "We have been insensible to well-meant criticism." We have felt hurt and called it heckling. The general response to Rethinking Missions is a case in point.

2. "We have made a god of the machine." We have "dug ourselves in" like the armies on the front line but there has been very little of "going over the top." We have delighted in statistics and determined to save the institution.

3. "We have shown a tendency to over-organize." Organs are necessary. And so is a vertebra to which we may attach our viscera. A disorganized body is pitiable as it progresses in the crowded street. We must have organization. But we may have too much of it.

4. "We have a tendency to go off after extreme theories."

We too easily align ourselves into camps with rival shib-boleths.

5. And lastly "we have lost our objective." We are so like the goat on the baggage car that ate the tag containing his destination.

After a few weeks in a pastorate so many questions arise that must be quickly referred for action that one takes the time to draw up his own chart showing the relationship of one department of work to all the rest.

TEMPORALITIES

A church has two functions, temporal and spiritual.

Once when Samuel Rutherford of Kidderminster was preaching on social issues and the dissensions of the time, he changed quickly to, "He's the Rose of Sharon, and the Lily of the Valley. There is a sweet scent in the heart of him who knows the Lord." From this praise of Christ he admonished his congregation to find their peace in Him. A laird in the audience whispered loudly, "Aye now ye're richt. Stay you there."

It sounds all right to say it so! But St. James said, "As the spirit without the body is dead so . . ." The church is a spiritual organization needing temporal paraphernalia and relationships.

To the Temporal will belong everything pertaining to the grounds, property and buildings. This includes, ushers, money, sexton.

The Spiritual functions of the church concern pastor and deacons. But—where does woman's work come in? And that of the Sunday school?

AN ERROR OF JUDGMENT

Once in the early days I noticed an absence of hymn boards in the Sanctuary. I ordered these, and when they had come, I asked the Sexton to hang them in the proper places.

"I can't do that," replied the sexton.

"Why not," I asked.

"I am forbidden to drive a nail or insert a screw without orders," was his firm reply.

I had supposed that if I presented the bill it would be approved. I saw then that I must be more careful. All I had wished to do was to save the time of busy men. But I blundered none the less. My act was interpreted, for one bad moment, as a subtle criticism of the business ability, or the artistic taste of one of my most important Boards. There is one text that it never does to ignore or overlook. "I magnify my office."

My organizational set-up when finished, looked like the one on the following page. It had not occurred to me before that an organization could be intricate.

NO ANTICIPATED CHANGES

Just as Vice-President Coolidge, on the death of President Warren G. Harding, announced that he would seek no immediate change in national policy, so, it would make for good will in any organization to proceed for a time with the existing organizational set-up.

But in the meantime study faithfully the By-laws under which the local congregation operates. When I enumerated my organizations, bodies, committees, and classes, I found ex-

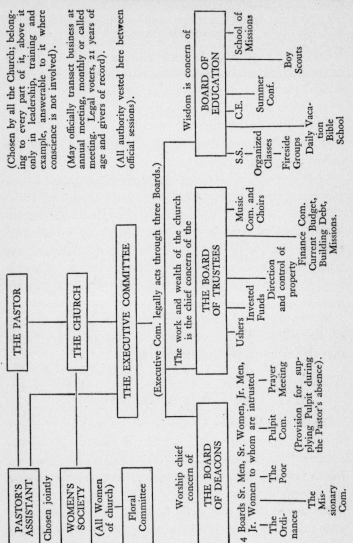

THE PASTOR

PASTOR'S ASSISTANT

Chosen jointly

THE CHURCH

(Chosen by all the Church; belonging to every part of it, above it only in leadership, training and example, answerable to it where conscience is not involved).

(May officially transact business at annual meeting, monthly or called meeting. Legal voters, 21 years of age and givers of record).

(All authority vested here between official sessions).

WOMEN'S SOCIETY

(All Women of church)

Floral Committee

THE EXECUTIVE COMMITTEE

(Executive Com. legally acts through three Boards.)

The work and wealth of the church is the chief concern of the

Wisdom is concern of

BOARD OF EDUCATION

S.S. — Organized Classes — Fireside Groups — Daily Vacation Bible School

C.E. — Summer Conf.

School of Missions — Boy Scouts

THE BOARD OF TRUSTEES

Ushers — Invested Funds — Direction and control of property — Finance Com. Current Budget, Building Debt, Missions.

Music Com. and Choirs

Worship chief concern of

THE BOARD OF DEACONS

4 Boards Sr. Men, Sr. Women, Jr. Men, Jr. Women to whom are intrusted

The Ordinances — The Missionary Com.

The Poor

Pulpit Com.

Prayer Meeting

(Provision for supplying Pulpit during the Pastor's absence).

actly 57. One mid-week I announced a meeting under the title of "57 varieties," and asked the head of each organization to be present and speak the briefest possible word of greeting.

When I went home from the meeting I took from the shelf Washington Gladden's *Christian Pastor*. Under the chapter heading, "Institutional Church," I found nearly all of these activities listed. How far the church has come in these brief years. Then men were debating if the church had any responsibility beyond the preaching function, and the Sunday School and Woman's work. All these other matters were open to debate. Now there is no church where all these are not a common place.

In June it will be found necessary to call these 57 heads together to arrange the calendar for the ensuing year and prevent overlapping and conflicts in dates. For while many dates are fixed yet the request for constant shifting is a grief until all meet together and agree upon the schedule. Thereafter, a Phillips Brooks church calendar * with blank squares filled with these assignments should hang in the foyer, and it must be understood that any organization may preempt a date merely by being the first to write their name on any remaining blank space throughout the year. But a rigid rule will need to be adopted to permit no revenue producing occasion to occur within two weeks of any of its rivals.

APPENDECTOMIES

There are always too many societies, some of them vestigial like the vermiform appendix and deserving excision with the surgeon's knife; but these must wait, the verdict of time.

---

* May be purchased of Samuel Ward Manufacturing Co., Boston, Mass.

Nothing survives unless it has what the French call a *"Raison d'etre."* When a function ceases wholly, the organ disappears, like the eyes of the fishes in Mammoth Cave; and opposition is the surest way to administer oxygen to a dying cause. The counsel of Gamaliel (Acts 5:38-39), must be for us here, "Let them alone; for if this counsel or work be of men it will come to naught."

Certain organizations for efficiency's sake should be united, or to economize God's good time. Others have long since ceased to perform any worthy function but continue under the laws of social agglutination. The only thing one can do is to husband time, and attend only those that by virtue of need demand our presence, if this can be done without ill feeling.

EDITOR

The files of the weekly church calendar may show it in need of editorial organization. One may begin there without harm. Let it carry the services of worship, Today, This week, and certain Notes. Congratulations for births and weddings, sympathy for deaths. In the field of illness one is in danger; make no effort to list these. It is impossible to include all, and where shall one draw the line?

The first annual meeting may be a nightmare of length and dreariness. But never again! The election of officers should be placed first, so that the tellers may perform their functions while the business proceeds. The reports may then be asked for and deposited unread with the clerk for editing and filing. Three reports should always be read in full: the pastor's report, the clerk's and the treasurer's. A speaker from out of the city should give an impassioned address of hope for the future.

The report of the election will be read; the officers installed, and refreshments served. The meeting should be completed within an hour and a half.

RECORDS

It is important to see how the members are recorded; received by Baptism, relation of Christian experience, letter, restoration; losses by death, letter, erasure.

When I get the consent of a person to join the church, if the church from which the letter is to come is slow in responding, we receive them pending the receipt of the letter. If the letter never comes, we record them as coming by experience. So we save both time and vexation.

I used to feel most impatient about the character of the membership. If they had membership in my church they must be spiritually minded. If not, their names should be erased. This was in line with the ancient practice of a strict discipline. Latterly, I have come to feel the cogency of Jesus' parable of the net. (Matt. 13:47-49.) I try to be careful in receiving members. After they are received, if they do not continue faithful, I ask my Official body to put the name of the erring, indifferent or lost one on an inactive list. For two years, I endeavor to win these back. After two years, if the condition continues, we cease to report such names to the denomination, or count them in making our reports. But we keep the Inactive list. And if at any time those on such a list, show an interest, or ask for a letter to another church, we restore the name to the original roll. Rarely have I been sorry for keeping a name on the list. I have been sorry for dropping one, too hastily.

THE PRESS

Early in every pastorate must come acquaintance with the local press. Furnish the newspaper with a glossy print costing about a dollar, but a picture which you and your parishioners approve. Learn to know the editor of the church page; furnish most carefully prepared copy, which obeys all the rules of the paper—and get the write-up there on time.

When one meets the reporter he may ask: "Tell me what makes one story good and the other unacceptable for your editor?"

He may say, "Gladly. First, put all the story accurately into the first paragraph. Each succeeding paragraph is less important. Be very careful as to your facts. Give correctly names and places and dates. Secondly, center your story about a person. Third, Proper margins; triple spacing; typewritten material written on one side of sheet only.

"Keep all editorial comment out of the write-up."

"WHAT DO YOU DO ALL DAY?"

"You always seem to be busy. What do you find to do? I thought a minister had one busy day in seven."

The refrain becomes so monotonous that at least once, one may introduce his sermon by answering after this manner, early in the year.

"You have been so interested in me and my conduct of the work this last year that for the sake of the younger folk who are here, I'm going to tell you how I spend every minute of my time, from one week's end to the other. You will observe by the Calendar, that every Sunday I am in the Study for prayer before the service, with my deacons. The morning service lasts till twelve, the Sunday School until one. I am always in the Young People's meeting at 6:00, I preach at 7:30. We will be home by nine p.m. unless we are invited out, as you so often have done for us. Monday is my sabbath. I try to keep it as such but with great determination and difficulty.

"Tuesday morning I am in my office. Tuesday noon I go to Rotary Club. Every afternoon but one until Friday I call at the homes of the congregation unless I have a funeral. Thursday morning I prepare for the prayer service that night. Saturday, I lock myself in for sermon preparation. I have no 'barrel,' and never shall have, as the term is used. You will see by looking at the calendar that there is some activity for me to attend every night this week, excepting Saturday. I do my studying from ten until midnight. I rise at seven every day."

CITY-WIDE CONTACTS

Early in every pastorate one must take a pad of paper and set down upon it, the list of organizations within the city with which he either is or should be acquainted, or on good terms.

All other churches.

The ministers union.

The Press.

The School System.

The Fraternal organizations.

The Patriotic organizations.

The Temperance organizations.

The Political organizations.

The Philanthropic organizations.

The Mortuaries.

The Hospitals.

The Service Clubs.

The penal and reformatory institutions.

The Y.M.C.A. and Y.W.C.A.

The Colleges.

If one is to continue as pastor in a community he must touch, know and mold all of these. Within twelve months, without urging yourself upon them you will have spoken before every one of these and possibly also before the colored church; the amalgamated Labor Unions of the city; and the shop girls at the Y.W.C.A. on a Sunday afternoon. Keep the list and check against it as rapidly as you make a contact. If your friends know of your desire to meet and speak before these groups they will assist you. No man seeks these audiences, to be seen and heard of men. But one must never forget that a part of his function is to the city at large.

The office of pastor of a local congregation becomes the agency through which he exercises this larger ministry. Some of these contacts are fraught with danger.

One feels like a person picking up two ends of a live wire, letting the voltage go through his body. Some will think us simply seekers after notoriety. To some we are Bolsheviki. The Unions at first may think we have been bought by the well-to-do, to come and placate them. The employers may wish we would let their troubles alone. Even our own church people may have their doubts.

There are many who are familiar with the gospel of personal salvation who do not see the relation, implicit in Christ who promised ultimate world triumph; except it come by catastrophe. We do ourselves no favor, nor our Lord, when we divorce the two elements of personal and social salvation.

They are both there. The Irish barrister stood before the bench defending a prisoner in the dark days when justice was most dear. When he insisted upon the law and the evidence and the rights of man there was a clatter of arms in the outer hall, intended to intimidate him. Looking the bewigged Lord Justice in the eye he said, "You may kill me if you will, but you cannot frighten nor silence me."

The task of preaching to all these groups is simply the necessity of being a true man. We have a message to deliver and must give it to "every creature." What people think of it, is beside the point and a begging of the issue, as Jonah learned in his day.

VII

THE DIGNITY OF WORSHIP

"But the hour cometh, and now is, when the true wor-
shippers shall worship the Father in spirit and in truth:
for the Father seeketh such to worship him."—*Jesus*
(*John 4:23*).

VISITORS at the New York World's Fair must have noticed the
title of this chapter over its Hall of Religion. I am using it to
direct your mind to the dignity of Christian worship.

The worship of the true God as recorded in Scripture from
earliest times has been highly conventional. Even in the days
of the unhewn stone altar there was required:

1. A perfect sacrificial offering. (Gen. 4:3; 8:20.)
2. Prayer.
3. Hope of Deliverance from sin.

The elements continue in the recorded accounts of Moses
and the Tabernacle; and take on an ornate character in the
Temple of Solomon with the addition of Song, musical in-
struments, religious symbols, incense, and robed processional,
(1 Kings 7 & 8). After the days of exile, this was of necessity
changed under Ezra (read Ezra & Nehemiah, Neh. 8:4). But
not of desire, but of the necessities of poverty, (Hag. 2:3).

In Jesus' day conventional worship was retained with an
orderly ritual, and He scrupulously attended its observance,
(Luke 4:16), on the Sabbath, and the more ornate services of
worship in the Temple five times per year. (Luke 2:41. John
4:45; 6:4; 7:10; 10:22.)

It was this attention to the Feast of the Passover that took Him to Jerusalem at the time of his crucifixion, (John 12:12). In spite of this historic groundwork which none can gainsay, the development of liturgy in Protestantism has been an autumn fruit slow to ripen, and rather hard and sour.

Romanism so set its stamp of fear upon the early New England congregation that worship consisted of little more than the singing of a metrical version of a psalm, a prayer, and the sermon of endless duration. The rigors of a New England winter did the rest. The order of worship, therefore, getting off as it did to a bad start has been a very slow growth.

The New Testament, nevertheless, indicates that first century Christianity was not informal. The worship of God then, seems to have included at least ten elements:

1. Attendance upon the meeting of the congregation on the sabbath. (Luke 4:16, John 20:19, 26.)
2. Hymns. (Eph. 5:19-32.)
3. Scripture Reading. (Luke 4:17.)
4. Prayer. (Acts 20:36; 1:14; 2:42.)
5. Offerings of Substance. (1 Cor. 16:20.)
6. Sermon. (Luke 4:19-20.)
7. The Ordinances. (Acts 2:41-46.)
8. Exhortation. (Acts 2:14.)
9. The Spiritual Attitude of mind. (Rev. 1:10.)
10. Invitation to Accept Christ as Savior. (Acts 2:37-38.)

These Biblical citations are not given as authoritative proof texts, but as representing the atmosphere in which worship is set forth in all authentic pictures of the day. They may be supplemented many times over. Paul embodied all of these elements in his services. The Reformers, Calvin, Luther,

Zwingli, Melancthon, all utilized the elements named in their liturgies.

It is surprising to see how closely the essential parts, of the mass in Catholic churches, consist of these elements we have named, cleverly combined with the Cross, and the Last Supper and dramatization. But these they are.

It would seem that both Protestants and Catholics feel forced back to these basal parts by the very needs of one's spiritual nature. To these elements which appear as basic, have been added in some services of worship a recital of the creed where desired and the Gloria. It seems not to be generally understood that the only proper place for the Gloria historically is following the Psalm or Responsive reading and to be sung standing. If one asks why, the only answer is "It is the custom." "As it was in the beginning." Protestants if they are to cling to some such ritual of worship as this will do well to beware of harsh criticism of ritual anywhere provided only that it does not sink into pure formalism, its chief danger.

It is not difficult to see how and why liturgy developed as a spectacle. Given a warm country, a congregation before the days of the loud speaker, too large for the human voice to reach, and one can see how some appealing form would be worked out that centralized upon the Crucifixion and the Last Supper. The Mass is a blend of both. We are interested in it not in praise or blame but in understanding; that we may order our own worship aright. If there is any Protestant equivalent for the high moment among Romanists when the host is elevated, it is in the pastoral prayer. Then the Catholic is very sure heaven and earth meet. We know it is so with us in a pastoral prayer. And our congregations must not be allowed to forget it.

The Pastor must make his congregation know this, feel it and look for it. Instead of the "long" prayer it should be the most inspiring moment of all. While the prayer will run through the well known groove of adoration, thanksgiving, confession, petition, supplication and back to final laudation, again, it must be spontaneous and alive. This requires health, vigor, sanity, imagination, sympathy. A constant saturation with the Scriptures and their memorization, familiarity with hymnody, chasteness of style, and a memorization, of many great prayers, helps. Prayers are never repeated. They are prayed. They arise out of need. They are clamorous with faith. The man who prays is a praying man who has prayed much alone. He knows the path. With God, he is on good terms. He does not plan it. But as he thinks of the absent loved ones, he says, "Though sundered far by faith we meet, around one common mercy seat."

A mind that is richly stored can do this. Little by little your people will come to love the moment of prayer.

The use of the Lord's Prayer is to be encouraged but the pastor should ascertain what form is used by the congregation; and when serving an outside group might say "we shall join at the close in the Lord's Prayer using the form 'forgive us our debts.'"

In general prayers that are read are not native to the evangelical faith outside a few communions and are not to be encouraged except in their native soil. They indicate the same poverty of spirit one finds in a ranter's prayer, or in one that is vainly repetitious. How easily we place the person who prays, "and now blessed Jesus, we just come to thee and we just claim the blessing, and we just wait for the promise." Or the other who says "and now again we come to thee and we pray that when the day is done is may be said of us, it was good to be in the house of the Lord." Or still another who recites "Almighty and ever livin' and lovin' God we bow before thee, before whom angels veil their faces, while the shadows of the evenin' are gatherin'."

It is too much to say that they do not pray. They do, and often in devout fashion. But prayers may easily become devoid of life and be only a mind-set, a pattern of the long ago. This is what Samuel Butler was protesting against in *The Way of All Flesh* when Ernest said that family prayer left him feeling like a honey bee that had vainly tried to gather sweetness from a painted flower on the wallpaper. Prayer must not be long or tedious. One will watch his own mood. Whitfield said "You prayed me into the Spirit and you prayed me out of it."

In congregational singing we suggest the singing of the entire hymn. Improvement in song will come by encouraging all, both in praise and censure. Choose hymns that have familiarity and inheritance value, or that can be quickly learned and have beauty and dignity. If a new hymn is sung, it should be sung regularly at every service for a month. Hymns should be appropriate to the theme. Eschew hymns or verses that are outmoded, or that teach a wrong idea;

> "Hark from the tombs, a doleful sound!
> My ears attend the cry!
> Ye living men come view the ground,
> Where ye must shortly lie,"

is gone forever let us hope.

Spend an evening once a quarter with some of the great hymns of the Christian faith.

"I have oftentimes tho't, that the heaven sent beam
Which the patriarch saw in his lonely dream,
Was a ladder of song and that there might appear,
Old Hundred, Balerma or Patmos or Mere."

There is a growing and wholesome feeling in all churches that the choir should be gowned. The Geneva gown is Protestant, not Catholic, in origin. It is a workman's smock. The Soutane or cassock, the long close fitting black garment buttoned in front worn by the Roman clergy is something quite different. The choir gown does away with a clash of color and competition or comparison in dress. A choir should be as large as possible and of four parts. If young it will need counsel about devout behavior. For this reason and to assist in robing junior choirs should have a choir mother. The processional in which the choir marches into its place singing the first hymn as a signal for the congregation to rise and join, has everything to recommend it.

A good choir must have numbers, ability and a Christian purpose. But an able singer requires only ability, and this sometimes goes with a difficult temperament. Thus the tradition persists through the years in regard to church choirs. Fortunate, the pastor who can claim a choir in which genius is wedded to grace and godly behavior.

The choir if of any size should have an organization with President, Librarian, Treasurer, Secretary, Organ Director and Chaplain. One of the deacons may act as chaplain but he should be chosen by the organization. Cultivate the social life of your choir with a mid-winter supper which the church gives them as a token of love, adding to this a summer outing.

THE CHILDREN

There has been much shifting of opinion in the past few years over building a liturgy of worship that will interest youth. The first phase of this was in a day when the family all went to church and sat together. The second phase came with the children's sermon. The third phase came when the children of a certain age were excused after the children's sermon and were sent to the vestry for a children's church. Many parents complained at this, and it was found that this practice rather hastened the permanent divorce of the children from the worship than retarded it. Many churches are still experimenting with a combined service. Some churches seem to have solved the problem with the children's choirs. The Young People's meetings and the church school retain their own character. And the youth are made to feel that they are an integral part of the regular worship, at least at the morning service. Their singing of a special number is as much a part of the service as any other. They are needed. They are robed and so they stay throughout the service. The pastor will be mindful of them. No sermon should be beyond the understanding of a twelve year old. It is not necessary to talk down to them. They are alert. Let them look up to you.

It is always safe for the pastor and the choir director to talk together about the service of the succeeding Sunday not later than Tuesday morning. By this time, the sermon subject has been chosen, and the hymns and special numbers can be chosen.

THE ORDINANCES

It is not the purpose of this chapter to discuss the various methods of observing the ordinances in the various denominations. That is impossible. We insist only upon each pastor familiarizing himself with the accustomed form in his communion until it becomes worshipful; that he have it so completely memorized that he is not its slave but its master; and that he approach it so reverently that it should in very truth be an avenue of grace to the recipient. If the administrant is young and unaccustomed to the office, usually some much older man will be found who is willing to share with him all the information that the ordinance requires.

An unordained cleric or layman may by vote of the church in certain Churches administer the ordinances. The time or frequency of administration of the Lord's Supper is usually determined by the local congregation or the custom of the denomination. Preparation for the observance of the Lord's Supper is customary and proper. This may be done in a Covenant meeting, in which the covenant vows of membership are reaffirmed or in preparatory services. The essential idea of every such service should be that though much of evil clings to us contrary to our desire, the Lord will cleanse us and make of us saints even yet, if we seek and ask His aid.

Even among churches known as "close communion" the practice is increasingly prevalent of giving an invitation which makes it apparent that all who feel themselves to be in Spiritual fellowship with Christ are eligible to the table regardless of denominational lines. The administrant at the Table is not a dictator and cannot determine who shall come.

THE LORD'S SUPPER

The Lord's Supper must be made more worshipful. It is amazing to find the Ancient Order of Free and Accepted

Masons putting so much of care into their liturgy, and in contrast our churches tending to perform their most sacred-ordinance so sloppily. Long hours of practice and perfect understanding with those who assist at the table should provide a technique of grace and beauty. If the elements are passed let those who serve be clad alike, in agreed upon garments. Let them repair to their stations during the singing of a hymn. Let them be seated by signal together. The giving of the Right Hand of Christian Fellowship or Confirmation or dedication of Children may take place at this point. Then the fellowship offering usually used for the relief of distress in the parish may follow so that the last impact of the service is not commercial. Then a silver laver and a faultlessly laundered napkin are available on a nearby small taboret or table for use by the ministrant before he handles bread to be consumed by the congregation. In most churches today the loaf or wafer has been cut or broken, except a small portion for symbolic use. The pastor begins "For I have received," I Cor. 11:23. As he says "And when he had given thanks he brake it," he adds "Let us pray." He hands the trays of bread to the deacons, with the charge "Take, eat, this is my body," etc. Upon their return to the table they will hold the plates until these are collected and placed upon the table by the Chairman of the Board, who after the deacons are served by the pastor, will himself then serve the minister. The minister rises and says in the language of the third century and pre-served for us in many service books, "The body of our Lord Jesus Christ that was given for thee, preserve thy soul and body unto everlasting life. Take this in remembrance that Christ's body was given for thee and feed on Him in thy heart by faith with thanksgiving."

This formula does not teach any particular doctrine as to the bodily Presence. It does admonish us to "feed upon Him by faith." It is increasingly used by congregations of all denominations in all parts of the Protestant world.

The congregation partakes together. The moment of silent prayer is terminated by the Pastor's "Amen." After the same manner the distribution of the cup proceeds. No longer in these days of sanitary precautions is the individual cup thought an offense. Rather the contrary. When the minister is served he says, "Drink this in remembrance that Christ's blood was shed for thee and be thankful." A carefully instructed congregation will not deposit the cups till all do so together. Receptacles for cups are now usually lined with plush or rubber silencers, and paper cups are available of the appointed size at a small price.

The congregation rises and sings one verse of some familiar hymn. Some hymn must be agreed upon and always used for this moment. The assistants of the minister retire in solemn processional. The pastor then may dismiss the group with "And when they had sung an hymn they went out" or with an appropriate benediction.

One persistent obstacle to the Lord's Table is still found in many hearts. It is as old as the "Shepherd of Hermas" or the Epistle to the Hebrews (Heb. 6:4-6) and as young as the memory of the newest Christian who has just read Paul's "eateth and drinketh damnation to himself." (I Cor. 11:29.) The pastor should assure his communicants that the quickest way to prepare for a worthy communion is not by the path of self attained perfection, nor even by a consciousness of rectitude. It is by the path of contrition. "There is joy in heaven over one sinner that repenteth." "God, be merciful to me a sinner."

"Just as I am, without one plea,
But that thy blood was shed for me,
And that, thou bidst me come to thee.
Oh, Lamb of God! I come, I come."

BAPTISM

Baptism will be best observed at the beginning of the service. Thus the fear and curiosity will be kept at a minimum, and the worship of the day least disturbed. In the case of the afflicted, baptism may be administered on the occasion of a mid-week service. Surely a heart that is sympathetic and mindful of fear on the part of the recipient is the best ingredient for its administration. Self-possession in the pastor begets it in the candidate.

Membership in a church presupposes proper instruction; and an appearance before the appointed committee of the church at least, and usually before the church itself where a confession of faith in Christ should be given. Instruction in what the rite involves as to time and appearance and suitable printed information will be given the candidate on this occasion.

Baptism must be performed, in any church and under every condition, so as to produce the spirit of self-dedication in the mind of the observer. In any meeting house, the robing room and the water must be warm. Whatever the custom, it gains nothing when accompanied by fear or levity. Henry Ward Beecher could take a crying baby in his arms and say, "the sweetest music of heaven is that made by a child."

Here is the place where the administrator if ever, will be robed, his manner calm. It will add to the service if he can recite a few verses from Scripture without the book and hand to each candidate a flower at the close.

Perhaps he will be able also to add to the congregation, "It is done as the Lord commanded and yet there is room." Fervent invitation for others to follow in the new life is never out of place at a moment like this.

MARRIAGE

The service of marriage is safeguarded by the laws of the State. One of the first duties of a pastor upon accepting a pastorate will be to go to the city hall or the county building or the district court and learn the laws concerning marriage. It may be necessary to sign the minister's register, or take an oath or show one's ordination certificate. One should, of course, have some acceptable form of the service committed to memory. It will be well to have this typewritten and interleaved in the red bound prayer book one usually sees carried, as much the badge of a marriage service in many communities as a wedding ring. One will not find it necessary to refer to the book except on rare occasions. The minister owes the prospective bride the preceding evening of the marriage for a rehearsal if it is to be of social importance. Much time will be spent in the practicing of the wedding march but of equal importance it is to know the order of service and to learn the cues, and to see that one knows his exact place in the procession entering and retiring. If it is a brief service conducted in the pastor's study, the service may be somewhat shortened to a prayer, followed by the vows and the pronouncement.

It should be understood that the bride is the absolute dictator of what is right at a wedding, in every respect save the official pronouncement. It, therefore, follows that many services will differ. The minister owes it to the bride to know her exact wishes and scrupulously follow them, if it can be done. Usually some one makes a slight mistake. It would not be a wedding, if it were otherwise. Prepare the bride's mind for this. Her composure is essential.

The minister and the best man are, of course, two people who never under any circumstance indulge in the shameless pranks that mark so many weddings.

In case of a double ring service, the procedure is identical. The bride receives her ring first. I personally prefer the form favored by the Presbyterian Service book, to the more ancient, "With this ring I thee wed." The Presbyterian form reads, "This ring, I give thee, in token of my abiding love and everlasting loyalty."

In case the bride is ignorant of what is expected or in doubt of the procedure to be followed, only then, or in case of a quite informal service, is it proper to vouchsafe advice as to the way the service is to proceed.

DEDICATION OF CHILDREN

All people, even those not wishing for the baptismal rite, wish their children reared for God. A service dedicating the parents to this task and making of the congregation a corporate god-parent in the task, is now common in many churches.

Christmas, Mother's Day and Children's Day are the times for Dedication of Infants and Children. Each pastor should work out a service of his own. It should consist of some Scripture like that in the 18th or 19th of Matthew and should require responses from the parents pledging them to rear the children in the ways of God. After this a carnation with a suitably engraved or printed card bearing the assurance that the card is a token that on a given date the child was offered in dedication to the Lord, should be presented to the parent. Most of the details of such a service may be in the hands of the chairman of the Cradle roll who keeps a record of all births in the parish.

Here is a suggestive type of service:

"Do you desire that your children, when they reach accountable years may become faithful Christians and ingrafted into the body of Christ?"

"We do."

"Will you try constantly to train them in the ways of the Lord?"

"We will."

"This service is chiefly a dedication of you to the task before you as parents. Will you, the congregation, by your example and prayer do all in your power to assist these parents in these holy vows?"

"We will."

DEDICATION OF HOME

We are now on the eve of a demand for a suitable dedicatory service for the home.

We offer here a service which has been used with blessing. The pastor begins:

"And into whatsoever house ye enter first say, Peace be to this house. (Luke 10:5.)

"We are met in the name of God after whom every family in heaven and earth are named, (Eph. 3:15) and in the name of Jesus Christ who visited the home of Peter, (Mark 1:30-31), and there brought a great healing; and who visited the home of Jairus, (Mark 5:22), and raised the daughter to life; to dedicate this home to God and to pray for His blessing upon it and all those herein. Let us hear what the Scripture saith:

"Except the Lord build the house, they labour in vain that build it." (Psa. 127:1.)

"Honour thy father and thy mother; that thy days may be long upon the land which the Lord thy God giveth thee." (Ex. 20:12.)

"For this cause shall a man leave father and mother and shall cleave to his wife; and they twain shall be one flesh." (Matt. 19:5.)

"For I know him, that he will command his children and his household after him, and they shall keep the way of the Lord." (Gen. 18:19.)

"When thou buildest a new house then thou shalt make a battlement for thy roof." (Deut. 22:8.)

"And these words that I command thee this day, shall be in thine heart, and thou shalt teach them diligently unto thy children, and thou shalt talk of them when thou sittest in thine house; . . . and thou shalt write them upon the posts of thy house and on thy gates." (Deut. 6:6, 7 and 9.)

Addressing the husband, he shall ask:

What is your declaration?

Husband: "I wish by this act to dedicate my home to God."

Pastor: "Believe on the Lord Jesus Christ and thou shalt be saved and thy house." (Acts 16:31.)

Addressing the wife, he shall ask:

"What is your declaration?"

Wife: Reads Ruth 1:16-17.

Pastor: "Train up a child in the way he should go and when he is old, he will not depart from it." (Prov. 22:6.)

Or this: "But one thing is needful. And Mary hath chosen the good part that shall not be taken away from her." (Luke 10:42.)

If there are small children, ask: "And what is your declaration?"

Child: "And Jesus said, Suffer little children to come unto me and forbid them not for of such is the Kingdom of heaven." (Matt. 19:14.)

The pastor lays his hands in blessing upon them. (Matt. 19:15.)

If there are older children the pastor will then say: "And what is your declaration?"

Youth: "Then said I, lo I come; in the volume of the book it is written of me, I delight to do thy will, oh My God. Yea thy law is within my heart." (Psalm 40:7.)

The Prayer: Oh God, who hast made the home the foundation stone of society and who didst establish it as thy first place of worship and religious instruction, look upon this home in blessing today. Make it more than an abode. Make of it a threshold of heaven where are united hearts. Grant to each one who comprises this home, health and length of days to serve thee with joy; minds stored with high thoughts and precious memories; souls purchased by the grace of heaven; hands busily employed in all helpful labors; in the name of Jesus Christ, Amen.

Let some one then read Edward Guest's "It takes a heap o' livin'." If a homily is desired a text for it may be found in II Kings 4:16. The question as to the well being of the home, is one of the greatest that we can ask. That home is "well" where there is God and a righteous influence. Pray for your children and with them.

FUNERALS

The purpose of a funeral service is four-fold. It is proper for the minister to say at the outset, "We are met to hold this Christian service over the mortal remains of John Doe." The Scripture is followed by prayer and this by a few brief remarks. Music is optional. The purpose to be kept in mind is first to express our faith in God and in the future life; second, to offer assurance of comfort and sympathy to the bereaved; third, to give an opportunity in some worthy way to express one's appreciation for the deceased; and, finally, to summon every hearer to the stern and certain bar of destiny. We are mortal. We march toward a certain end. Live so that death loses its power and "is swallowed up in victory."

Each pastor should require of himself that he commit to memory at least a minimum of Scripture that may be used at any funeral under any conditions. This should include the following, in the order given. Deut. 33:27; Job 14:1-14, first clause; John 11:25; John 14:1-6; II Cor. 5:1-9. In addition to this one may use but need not memorize, in the case of very young children Matt. 18:1-6; Matt. 18:10, 11 and 14; Matt. 19:13-15; Zech. 8:5; Isa. 40:11.

At the graveside the pastor stands at the head of the grave. It is easy to remember this. He stands there as if he spoke for one who could speak for himself no more. If in doubt, one may always ask the sexton or undertaker which is the head. The custom for the undertaker or minister to scatter the petals of a broken flower on the remains is today well-nigh universal. But one Scripture is appropriate for the closing prayer at a graveside. It is found in Hebrews 13:20 and 21.

Some committal form is desirable. If one's mind will permit

the use of the ancient forms of the Prayer or Service Book all is easy. If not, one must rewrite this formula until it does honestly say what one's heart feels; and then commit it to memory.

Some will be satisfied with a poem or a brief prayer or the twenty-third Psalm. Over President Garfield's body this was recited:

> "He has fallen asleep,
>   He is resting at last.
>   The heart has grown still,
>   And the fever has passed.
>   He suffers no longer in heart or
>   in brain;
>   And the fever that racked him,
>   shall not come again.
>   He is fallen asleep,
>   And the fever is passed.
>   Thank God as you weep,
>   He is resting at last."

When the service is over, one will go immediately to the chief mourner, and say a personal word, before the group leaves the cemetery.

Funerals are often held in the worst of weather. In those cases, the pastor is within both his rights and his duty who says, "It will be thought no discourtesy to the dead, if I insist that no one removes his hat. Please remain covered."

41741

VIII

THE WEEKLY PRAYER MEETING

How tedious and tasteless the hours,
When Jesus no longer I see.
Sweet prospects, sweet birds and sweet flowers,
Have all lost their sweetness for me.
The mid-summer sun shines but dim;
The fields strive in vain to look gay;
But when I am happy in him,
December's as pleasant as May.

"The prayer meeting is the thermometer of the church" is one of those universally accepted proverbs that is wrong. It is rather the thermometer of the day in which we live. It is our most aggravating and persistent problem. Some older people enjoy it and are hyper-critical that others do not. There seems no way of breaking an age-old tradition that the choir and several other organizations shall meet on the same night; and so draw off much cream from the top of the bottle. Even an adjustment and division of hours for the evening does not effect a correction. Both groups will continue, critical of each other. This brings us to an examination of the whole problem. The mid-week service is needed for both social and spiritual reasons. Its scope must be the lifting of the emotions; instruction in prayer, Bible study and missions; and there must also be given an opportunity for self-expression. Perhaps, here is a place for a church question box.

One must guard against queer people. One, too, is always

101

faced with the danger of unbridled, non-constructive criticism. Begin by choosing and enlisting an able pianist. Then look about for an able song leader. Next secure a gifted woman to come in the afternoon and put a homey, decorative touch in the arrangement of chairs and platform.

For the first six weeks of autumn send out post card invitations to every church member, mailing one sixth of the whole each week, in alphabetic succession. About one in ten will respond. On October fifteenth, begin a series of six missionary programs. Secure a special speaker and pay the expenses if need be out of your own pocket. Ask one of the organized classes to take as its share of the labor, the issuance of invitations to various organizations on successive nights, and also to serve light refreshments at the close. This will bring twenty to fifty more. During the Christmas holidays make no especial effort to maintain attendance; but during the week of prayer, arrange a meeting with youth from eighteen to twenty-five years of age for Tuesday; with the men for Wednesday; the women for Thursday; and invite the entire church for Friday night. The following week, arrange for prayer meetings at the four compass points of the city in the homes of members, and arrange also for an afternoon service for the aged and infirm, bringing them to the church in automobiles. Some of this accretion you may be able to keep.

For the following four weeks give serious studies of great Bible books. These always prove popular. During March consider "How one enters the new life with God." This, in preparation for the Baptism that one hopes may occur near Easter. Surprisingly, this will bring out many warm hearted people who wish an evangelistic touch, and who have been critical of you because they have not found it.

My friend, Dr. Atwater, of the Episcopal Church held a service to which were invited many who were not familiar with the usage of that church, in which he explained the symbolism, usage and procedure of a liturgical service. It met with great favor. We never lose time in explaining the things that seem to us rudimentary. "How does one enter the Christian life?" "Master, what must I do to inherit eternal life?" "What must I do to be saved?"

Many are still seeking the answer. "Repent, believe and confess Christ."

"Yes, I hear you, pastor; but what do these things mean?"

"Repent?"

"Believe?"

"Confess?"

After Easter invite the new members to attend the midweek service and give them careful instruction in church duties. At each of these services be careful to have instructed members speak an informative word about the various organizations and interests; the Lord's Supper, when and how; the denominational journals; the Women's Society; the Church School; the Finances.

On the evening of the Thursday before Easter, the night of the institution of the Supper, hold a communion service. The candidates should be baptized on the Sunday before, so as not to impede the Easter service. A processional may be formed. First, the choirs; then, the new members. Seat them in front for the Right Hand of Christian Fellowship. Then, the Deacons; Pastor, at the rear. The church will be filled. I have never seen it fail. They have been instructed before, that this is an anniversary service, of much more moment to us than Christmas. "On the same night in which our Lord was betrayed." The congregation will sing "All hail! the power of Jesus' name." The hand of fellowship is given. The emblems are given and taken, and the meeting is dismissed. It is one of the high points of the year, almost equalling Easter in interest.

During May the pastor will continue as before, only now the major interest will be the Christian Home. "Bring your home problems. Let us discover how Christ would have us build our home life." The months of June, July, and August should be placed in charge of the elders and Deacons. The mid-week meeting that began as a sorry failure with no more than fifteen in attendance, and that everyone said could not be maintained, will now have an average attendance of forty-five.

QUESTIONS

A neighbor will hear of its success and come in to enquire, "But how do you get those who attend to take part?"

Sometimes I ask a question. "What is the story, the key word, the main thought of this Book?" Sometimes I give them a stereotyped phrase that all may repeat singly or in chorus. Sometimes I give them a specific thing to pray for. Sometimes I remind them, "if two of you shall agree" (Matt. 18:19). And when a cause of prayer has been presented, I ask agreement. Often this secures several prayers on the same matter. Always we pray for the sick, by name, if their case is presented. Once a month we hold the briefest sort of a business meeting. Always we devote the entire mid-week service, ten days before Easter, to receiving new members. That is the dead line. It takes the entire evening to hear their declarations of faith.

"Do you find it possible to break the old of their meaningless cliches in prayer?" is asked.

No; not if you let them pray as they will; "Pray only for this one thing, please."

"Do you keep the service informal?"

Very!

"Do you announce the topic?"

Always!

"Why do you encourage people to participate?"

Chiefly, for their own training. William James used to say that "there is no reception of ideas without some corresponding expression and vice versa." We have, therefore, to encourage expression. If I can get a person to say in my service even so simple a statement as "I love Jesus," or "I want to be like Jesus," or "I will pray daily this week," I've done something for him of value.

"How long is the service?"

Exactly one hour. I close promptly. Sometimes I say, "There are only ten minutes remaining but that gives time for twenty more to speak. The service is better for us both if you have a part." Or, "Let us hear from one who never took part before." Always before we close, we take time for introduction of strangers. Sometimes we close with a circle of friendship around the room, clasping hands and repeating together the Lord's Prayer.

"But, don't you find many faults of public prayer?"

Yes. Familiar prayers, prayers of fear, elocution, length, pet phrases, pious tones, smartness, polemic, and insincerity.

"Well, then, you said you never called on anyone to pray, always leaving it to one's own spiritual impulse; how do you get them to participate?"

Sometimes I wait. Sometimes I say: "I want five to lead. Who will lift their hands? When five are ready we will begin."

"But how do you nurture your own prayers?"

By much reading of the devotional parts of Scripture. By committing hymns and appropriate poems to memory. By considering my own needs and that of my congregation. By praying.

Here are a few of the subjects considered for the prayer service as they come at random.

TOPICS FOR PRAYER SERVICE

The story of how and when you gave your heart to Christ. (Make it brief.)

What probably happened at Pentacost. (Be realistic.)

My part in this church.

The goal I want my church to reach.

How I know I'm a Christian.

One thing I'm praying for.

Things that have hindered me in prayer.

The central facts of my creed.

The book of Scripture I like best.

The hymn I like best.

The chapter I like best.

I thank God for what?

One thing I got from last week's prayer service.

Jesus' prayer life.

When do people pray?

Story of George Mueller.

Do I want my prayers answered?

Job in prayer.

Peter in prayer.

Elijah in prayer.

Abraham in prayer.

The rule of prayer in the book of James.

The apostle I would like to have been.

Does it pay to pray?

My favorite missionary.

My favorite mission field.

A prayer meeting for the official family of the church.

A prayer meeting for our Sunday School.

Is a prayer meeting Biblical.   (Acts 16:13.)

Last Sunday's sermon.

Is it right for Christians to accumulate wealth?

Go to war?

Join a Union?

Play cards?

What I would do for Christ if I had a million dollars?

Family prayer.

Jacob and prayer.

Moses.

Nehemiah.

One thing have I desired!

If I had but one prayer to pray.

If I had but one testimony to give.

ANSWERS TO PRAYER

Sackville West in his *Joan of Arc* has a page in which he says that while he is not an orthodox believer, he is obliged to think that sometimes God breaks through in some unusual manifestation, to unusual individuals. God did this in the case of Jesus, Joan, Francis of Assissi and Paul of Tarsus, he believes.

Some day the psychologists will tabulate authenticated cases. Why should not we do book-keeping on what seem to be demonstrated answers to prayer in our experience or observation? In four years I have had four cases.

CASE ONE

A motorman, not a member of the church, was taken seriously ill, and remained so for many weeks. One night he and his wife suddenly appeared in the prayer service and at the time of testimony quietly reported without hysteria this incident.

"Last Wednesday night, I couldn't sleep. I asked God for the first time in my life if I would live or die, and, if possible, to let me live, for Christ's sake. A voice spoke and said, 'You will live. I will give you a sign; listen.' Almost at once there was a loud rap on what seemed to be the closed bedroom door. My wife awoke and said, 'What was that?' I said 'It's God. Listen.' The knock was repeated twice more. I heard three raps. My wife heard two. We both arose and examined the house from cellar to attic, but there was no human in sight. In the light of the experience, we have done the only thing we know. We've given ourselves to Christ and ask for church membership." They were baptized and are still faithful members of a non-hysterical type.

It is now four years after the event, and a thousand things had overlaid it in my mind when the motorman appeared in my study the other day. He is still one of my most faithful and devoted members. He sat down and drew a deep breath.

"Do you know, pastor, I work with machines so much that I believe in cause and effect. And I could never understand about those raps on my bedroom door. But I've got it all figured out. I'll bet it was the horse in the stable next door. I think I was almost dreaming, but didn't know it. And the horse aroused my subconscious mind."

"Well, does it disturb your faith, Jim?"

"Disturb it? Not at all. God spoke to Baalam by an ass, didn't he? If God wanted to bring a motorman to church by horsepower, it's all right with me."

And after a moment, he reflected: "It's funny that I hadn't ever thought about that horse before."

"But Jim, if you had, perhaps you'd never have come."

He laughed heartily and said, "You're right, pastor; you're always right."

CASE TWO

An English textile worker, profane, and drunken was the father of a young man twenty years of age, who was active in the Christian Endeavor Society. One day he said to his father, "Please come to church with me tomorrow, Dad?"

The father in a violent rage replied, "Shut your mouth! I'll never cross the door of that church nor that of any church."

The boy quietly said, "Yes, you will! You'll come," and went into the house and told his mother. Together they prayed for the father's conversion. On the following Saturday, they buried the young man of a ruptured appendix. The father today is a total abstainer and one of the most active members of his son's church. He gives no signs of being abnormal. He rarely speaks of his son's death; but when he does, he says, "God had to hit me in my tenderest spot to knock sense into me." If a man says to him, "But God didn't kill your son, did he?" he quietly replies, "My son isn't dead. Wherever he is, he's working hard for God. Count on that."

CASE THREE

A clergyman of a neighboring church came into the study and said, "My four leading laymen have asked me to sever my relations as pastor, and I have nowhere to go."

"Why?"

"It's partly my fault. I suppose I have been too sharp and not sufficiently tactful in my admonitions."

"What charge do they bring against you?"

"Only one; incompatibility."

"Will you fight it?"

"No!"

"Why not?"

"The man who fights dismissal, usually divides a church, and becomes a marked man."

"What will you do?"

"Nothing, but pray!"

That was in September. The next May he received a telegram inviting him to a pulpit, a thousand miles away, at no reduction in salary.

CASE FOUR

This time it was to me that the experience came. I was dismissing a service, when a nurse from the hospital across the way came rushing to me saying, "You must come quick. They have sent for you."

I was met at the door by another nurse who hustled me into a surgeon's apron and face mask. In the slow moving elevator, was the most skilled surgeon of the area, a professor in the University Medical School, a devout Catholic. He explained: "One of your girls in the church has had an accident. She is bleeding to death, probably. She is in a state of shock. Too much time has elapsed, already. If she is saved, it will be by my knife and your prayers, but mostly by your prayers. Please pray for me as I operate, and for her."

The incision was made. The skilled hands examined every organ. "It isn't here, nor here." At last came,—"here it is." His fingers brought up a shattered spleen, the most friable tissue in the body. Without turning his head, the physician reached out his hand and took from the nurse the curved needle, inserted it and drew tight the suture.

"If ever you prayed, pray now," the surgeon urged. And I prayed not only that God would guide the hand of the physician but that God's will would be done.

Forty-eight hours later, the surgeon and I stood again, together, above her pillow. "She'll live!" was his verdict.

She smiled wanly and said, "You've always said, 'all you need is Christ,' but I've said 'Christ and much else,' but now I can say, 'Thou, Oh Christ, art all I want.'"

Six weeks went by, every day marking an improvement in her condition, and then one night she stood in prayer meeting, and for her first testimony recited the following poem by an author unknown to me.

> The world I thought belonged to me—
> Gods, gold, people, land and sea—
> Where e're I walked beneath God's sky,
> In the old days my word was "I."

Years passed: There flashed, my pathway near,
The fragment of a vision dear:
My former word no more sufficed
And what I said was "I and Christ."

But, O, the more I looked on Him
His glory grew, while mine grew dim;
I shrank so small, He towered so high
All I dared say was "Christ and I."

Years more the vision held its place,
And looked me steadily in the face;
I speak now in an humble tone
And what I say is "Christ alone."

—Author unknown.

IX

YOU'LL FIND HIM AT THE CHURCH OFFICE

"Jesus answered, are there not twelve hours in the day."—*John 11:9.*

"We must work the works of him that sent me while it is day. The night cometh when no man can work."— *John 9:4.*

IT IS necessary that one have a room at home in which is a desk, some books, and a telephone; and here one will spend much time in study and preparation on certain evenings and on Saturdays; but I will not let my home be made into a business house for the transaction of church business. The church study must be at the church, and the pastor must have regular office hours. It is the only way to insure, and the only way to preserve, privacy in one's home.

OFFICE HOURS

Thereafter, one should be in the church office from nine A.M. to twelve noon, from Tuesday to Friday. Every afternoon is spent in pastoral calling. Someone will be found, either a paid assistant, or a volunteer, who will keep the office open and answer the phone until five. If no room exists in the church as an office, one should be built, book shelves installed, a toilet and wash stand constructed, and a large closet built in for holding the paraphernalia of a business office.

A telephone with an extension to the vestry should be wired with a switch so that the conversation may be private, if required. An odorless, gas-proof, heater can be installed, for days when the church is not otherwise heated.

EQUIPMENT

A flat top desk, typewriters, chairs and a good desk light must be secured for a stenographer's use, and a companion desk for the pastor. The church may not feel at once able to employ a stenographer and office assistant but there are always childless, married women, of known piety and character, perhaps former private secretaries, whom one could engage at practically little expense. The Woman's Society will provide a rug and drapes for the windows. One should also purchase inexpensive steel filing cabinets. There should be three of them, with four drawers each, 14″ x 24″ x 52″, the standard size, and manila filing folders, straight cut, 9 points thick, 9″ by 11¾″ for 8½″ x 11″ paper. One of the cabinets will be used for sermons, one drawer for correspondence, and one for clippings.

FILING SYSTEM

Sermons should be numbered serially but kept in at least four separate drawers for morning, evening, Sunday school and mid-week services; a fifth drawer may be employed for funeral addresses, and a sixth for addresses before special bodies. At first this may seem laborious, but by the time one's addresses have reached two hundred at the end of the first year, the wisdom of the system becomes apparent.

These sermons and addresses each bearing a serial number

must be tabulated also on 3″ x 5″ cards. I make out five of these cards for each address. One, the serial number card giving number, subject, place and date of delivery. The second card I file by date, the third by text, the fourth by subject, and the last by alphabetical arrangement. My latest serial number is 3982. I can tell you in less than a moment where any address may be found, when and where preached, and the response it elicited. This file has cost me very little time, but I know constantly whether I am repeating myself.

BOOKS

My available funds for books are small and the demands upon them are heavy. What books should one purchase? What can I afford? One is wise to keep his college and Seminary textbooks. These include the complete works of most of the English and American classic poets, probably an excellent four-volume church history, a good unabridged dictionary, and a concordance. One may always secure also two volumes on Religious Bodies issued by the Census Department at Washington, D. C., and sent by one's Congressman on request. One may purchase a full set of standard encyclopedias, and a four volume set of the latest Bible dictionary for about $125.00. When purchased these are a lifetime possession and pay for themselves many times over. It used to be said that there was no good one volume Bible commentary. This is no longer true. There are now several. If one wishes to make a more ambitious outlay, the Cambridge Bible is still regarded as scholarly and up-to-date by nearly all students.

CLIPPINGS

The clipping file becomes an invaluable mine of ore, and from its raw material one continually enriches his messages. One will be surprised to see the files that fill the most rapidly. They become barometric.

Bible.

Biography.

Brotherhood.

Childhood.

Christmas.

College.

Denominational.

Easter.

Economics.

Education.

Evangelism.

Facetiae. (I find it difficult to remember or tell well, a humorous story, and so I preserve the best that I hear. I use these sparingly).

Hymns and their stories.

Illustrations.

Liquor.

Minister.

Missions.

Money. (Here I have tabulated more than a hundred short stories, or bon-mots with drawing power to be told just before the offering for the Lord's work is taken).

Mother.

Music.

Prayer.

Sermons of others.
Racialism.
Ritual and Liturgy.
Thanksgiving.
War and Patriotism.
Women.
Young People.

PAYMENT OF BILLS

Receipted bills must be carefully treasured in a bill file for six years, until the law of the state declares a debt outlawed. Never let the tenth of the month pass until every bill is paid. "More men have been wrecked by debt than by any other single sin."

The first check will always be drawn to the Treasurer of the church. Unpaid bills, keep in a special pigeon hole, and all valuable papers in a safety deposit box, at the bank.

PERSONAL RECORDS

For the present and until one can afford a better, inexpensive plan, one may keep small blank books in a top drawer of the desk and in each of these make personal record of:

Church attendance.
Accessions by letter.
Baptisms.
Calls.
Dedication of babies.
Dismissals.

Financial Report of Collector (weekly).

Funerals.

Weddings.

At the first, too, one may content himself with a shoe box to hold his 3″ x 5″ cards. Later if one can afford it, have small drawers for these. And keep there:

Membership list of church.

Prospective members.

Sunday school by classes, and departments.

CHURCH ROLL

The church roll will be divided into *three* sections, the active, the inactive, and the non-resident. There will be many times when one will wish quickly to segregate these. This can be done, the more readily if the men's names are on a light buff card, the women's on white and children's (under fifteen) on a nile green.

On one's desk there should be kept a well annotated book containing the constitution of the church, another copy of the church roster much more easily consulted than a card index, a directory of the officers of each organization and a list of all Boards and Committees with the year of their expiration in office. Here also one keeps the Denominational annual, the City Directory, the Hymn book and the King James version of the Bible. This year's city directory is expensive. Therefore, I asked one of my business men for his, of last year. It serves my purpose, and saves money.

At my left on the desk I keep the file for next week's calendar, the material for which must be in my hand by Thursday morning at the latest. The church notes and advertising must be in the hands of the newspaper not later than Friday night at 6 P.M.

THE STUDY WALL

On my study walls I have hung with pride my diplomas from college and seminary and also an excellent copy of Hoffman's "Christ in the Garden of Gethsamane." Hanging where my eyes may always see it, I have placed my ordination paper. "Set for the defense of the Gospel." It is the shining mark for many a witticism. "Does the mighty gospel need the defense of weak man?"

"Webster says that a defense may be a friendly plea. One might offer that, even for the strong who were misunderstood—by cynics, shall we say—who derive their protection from its bastion."

My picador withdraws to a safe distance.

GOD SUPPLIES

On the wall in addition to the adornments already mentioned, my women have hung a lovely copy in color of Cologne Cathedral. The only other decoration on the wall seems to be a dollar bill in a gilt frame. It has a story. It was given me by a pastor's widow. Her husband dropped dead one night in the pulpit. She reared four sons. One, a clergyman; two, physicians; one, a school teacher. "And I did it on that." It reads, "I will not suffer my faithfulness to fail. Psalm 89:33. This certifies that the supply of all your need has been deposited in the Treasury of Heaven. My God shall supply all your need according to His riches in Glory by Christ Jesus. Phil. 4:19. Payable on request."

"Take it my son," she said, "you can bank on it. It's a blank check for you to fill in, already signed by the King of heaven." Later I purchased many copies of it from a publisher and distributed them* to my congregation, and preached on Matt. 8:26, "Why are ye fearful, Oh, ye of little faith?"

IMMUNITY

On my desk I keep my wife's picture prominently displayed. It is its own testimony and inspiration.

Because many matters of an intimate nature must be kept on record, the doors are always locked at night and the office is always open and accessible by day. A sign at the street door points the way. The main door into the office from the auditorium when I came contained a frosted glass pane. After a few days I requested that this be changed and plain glass substituted.

"My husband is away for a week. We have such a lovely room where you could rest. You are getting very tired. Everyone is remarking about it," was the invitation one day.

When my over-dressed and over-rouged visitor was gone, I called my assistant in and said, "My middle name is loyalty to God and my congregation. I never talk about anyone. And I do know the legal meaning of the phrase, 'a privileged communication.' If you don't, I want you to ask some lawyer to tell you. You are here because I trust you implicitly. But: ——, hereafter, I want you to remember three things well. I have no private mail. You are to open all my letters. Second, you are to listen in, with me on all conferences unless I spe-

---

* Excellent copies of these may be obtained from the Million Testament Campaign, 1505 Race St., Philadelphia, Pa.

cifically ask you to withdraw; and third, I am never 'in' to that woman again."

This relationship that one sustains to women was the concern of Paul as he wrote Timothy. (I Tim. 5:2.) "The elder women as mothers; the younger as sisters, with all purity."

One goes to a funeral, where the husband is laid away. As she turns from the grave, she throws her arms about you in despair. She even kisses your hand. St. Paul is telling you to take this woman as she means, and not try to take advantage even for a moment in your mind, of a broken or defenseless heart. Situations such as these are infrequent, but they or their equivalent must occasionally be met.

PRINTING AND OFFICE SUPPLIES

Ask the budget committee to include in the budget a small item to cover office expense, including all the usual necessary accessories to an office, also stamps, the printing of stationery, and the expense of a good mimeograph. The principal item on the printing bill will be the cost of the weekly church bulletin and a few other items, such as communion cards and tracts to be distributed in calling. There is always the need of something to encourage devotional reading in the congregation. For this need I have prepared "The Greatest Chapters," three hundred and sixty-five daily readings for use in family prayer.*

Cards must be printed for the every member canvass, and for new members to sign. On the following page is a card which for my work has proven itself effective:

---

* May be purchased of the American Baptist Publication Society, 1701 Chestnut Street, Philadelphia, Pa. Five dollars per hundred.

FIRST CHURCH

A Home in which it is a pleasure to give in Work-Worship-Wealth

---

I hereby commit myself to a regular subscription in favor of the First Church, which shall remain in effect until I notify Church Office otherwise: to be used for following purposes:

UNIFIED BUDGET (Missions   Weekly ......$..........
        Current Expense)   Monthly ......$..........

                                Yearly ......$..........

....

....

Date Effective .... Signature ....

And another card for the communion roll.

COMMUNION CARD   First Church

Name ....

Address ....

Remarks ....

....

    Please write your full name and address on this card. If you know of a member of the church who is ill, kindly note the fact, with any other item of interest, under "Remarks."

    Strangers communing with us will kindly state in full the name of the church where they hold membership. If you expect to make your home here, the pastor will be glad to know the fact, that he may call upon you.

Month ....   Year........

The communion card will be one's most effective source, for discovering changes in address which is the most persistent problem of any pastor, and one producing the saddest losses to any denomination.

One hundred post cards should be printed as follows:

```
                    FIRST CHURCH
                 Church and George Streets
                   Lowell, Massachusetts
  Dear Pastor:
      It is my intention to unite with the First Church of Lowell,
  Mass., under the pastoral leadership of Rev. A. M. Bailey.
      Kindly send him, at the above address, my church letter.
                            Faithfully yours,
  Date,
```

One must carry these with one wherever one goes and counsel one's personal workers to do so. Count the week lost in which one does not secure the signature of a stray member from another community.

CHURCH LETTERS

When the first snow falls one may say at the close of the sermon. "I have been wondering if my eyes deceive me. I do not think the white outside is snow. I think it is the white of those cold lost church letters of Protestants who have moved to this city. Whatever it is let's not grow cold in devotion. The reason people give me most often for not bringing a church letter is that they are uncertain of making this their residential city. There are people still here after ten years' residence who say they are not sure of staying. If one is to stay in a city for a month or more it is safe to unite by letter. It takes no more time than to draw or deposit a check. And one may always receive a letter within a week of the time it is requested."

Constant reminder seems the only hammer to batter down this wall of prejudice and neglect. The problem in most cases is to get them to make the decision to join. It may cost money.

WELCOME OF NEW MEMBERS

Each church publishing house probably carries a small booklet in an illuminated envelope containing instruction upon matters of faith, salvation, baptism, communion, service and giving. This will also contain a certificate of church membership. One of these booklets should be given to every new member. When a person comes before the membership committee he should be asked to sign the following card:

FIRST CHURCH
* Enlistment Card

It is my earnest purpose, upon becoming a member of the First Church, to aid, in every reasonable way I can in the successful carrying out of its program. To this end—

First—I shall make it my practice to be a regular attendant at the Church services.

Second—I shall be willing to serve in any capacity connected with the Church organization for which I am at all fitted.

Third—As a good steward of God, I hereby agree to contribute through the treasuries of the First Church—

For current expenses, the sum of..................$..........

For Missions the sum of.........................$..........

For the Building Fund, the sum of................$..........

Fourth—I faithfully promise to notify the church office in writing of every change in my address.

NAME ....

ADDRESS .... PHONE........

---

* This will be recognized as essentially the recommendation of Rev. F. A. Agar, D.D. of New York City, Church Efficiency expert.

Some pastors add to the above a fifth specification.

Fifth. Failure to keep the above promises over a period of two years, shall constitute a sufficient reason, for the removal of my name from the church roll.

Those who sign the above card should receive the following:

FIRST CHURCH

In recognition of the foregoing, we, the members of the First Church, covenant, on our part, to do all within our power to aid

....

in carrying out the purpose to which...........................
has subscribed.

Signed on behalf of the Church,

.... *Pastor*

.... *Deacon*

.... *Clerk*

When a person seems reluctant to sign, they should be told that when the signed card is returned the vote will then be taken in accordance with church rules. Allowance will, of course, be made for the very poor who wish to unite but are able to make no pledge. But almost any person who is able to join at all, should be able to make some payment so as to cover the requirement, "a contributor of record." In no case have I known it to alienate any person worthy of membership. We have all been too lax in our reception of new members. Having received them, what more can we do. The new members will come, like a skittish horse, to respect one who drives with a stiff rein.

HONOR ROLL

After this procedure has been in operation for a few months, it will become an accepted fact that a member of the church is a contributor of record, and at the close of each year, an honor roll may be displayed behind a locked, glassed frame giving the names, but not the amounts, of all those who pledged and paid in full for the year preceding. A few may grumble, but all will pay. The greatest care, however, is necessary in the preparation of the list. Usually, it should be displayed tentatively for several weeks, asking for correction before final typing. A word of admonition in the church bulletin may read, "Our books close in two weeks. The honor roll is about to be typed."

FILE THE SUNDAY BULLETIN

At the end of the year the calendars should be bound in duplicate and one copy kept by the church clerk and another by the pastor.

BEGGARS AND BUMS

Bums and beggars are quick to discover the way to our door. If a man applies for alms, he should be listened to and always given a quarter unless he has liquor on his breath, in which case, he may be told, "Please return when you have had no liquor." Repeaters should be asked from what parish they come, and referred while they are still present, by telephone, either to their own pastor or to the local police. Many, of course, impose upon this attitude, but it seems to be the toll exacted from us by virtue of our office. Most men do not beg unless they are hungry, or until drink has done its worst. A very few will come to our door who are the victims of illness, mismanagement and a ruthless industrial system. Whenever an imposter leaves our door, we may only smile and read again James 2:15-16. "There goes John Wesley but for the grace of God."

FLORAL DECORATION

If on one's first Sunday, a single flower in a bud vase adorns the platform, one may suggest to the Women's Society that a Floral Committee be created. A special floral calendar painted by a local woman of talent may be put in the vestibule.* In the calendar a line may read, "The flowers today are furnished by Mr. and Mrs. R. G. Brabrook in memory of their daughter, Flora, entered into rest." Soon, every Sunday of the year will be spoken for.

MOTTO CALENDAR **

In early September order copies of a motto calendar which the pastor and his wife may distribute on the Sunday preceding New Years day. The congregation, guided by the head usher, will march by the front of the auditorium and receive the wish for a happy New Year, while one's wife hands out the calendars. Calendars must contain no advertising. In the course of time this ministry becomes regarded almost as an essential expression of love by one's people.

---

* Plain black and white altar guild calendars for the flower committee may be found in nearly every denominational book store.

** Should be ordered at 1½ cents apiece from Zabel Bros., Fifth St. and Columbia, Philadelphia, Pa. not later than Sept. 1.

DISPLAYING THE FLAG

In every congregation there are those who wish to display the American flag, in the auditorium. This may be referred to one's official Board without recommendation, and the flag if placed should be at the foot of the pulpit platform on the right of the congregation and a Christian flag on the left.

Prominent on his desk one must keep the desk book for engagements, and every Tuesday morning he must check to see that it tallys with the church calendar.

In the foyer one will place a literature table with suitable periodicals on display, and nearby may be a church guest book.

No card entirely satisfies one, to use with those who wish to join the church, but the following is in wide use by several large evangelical bodies.

MY DECISION

1. I am not yet a professing Christian, but I WOULD LIKE TO BE. I decide today to forsake every known sin, and follow Christ. I do trust myself to God's forgiveness for the past, and to His power to help me for the future. It is my purpose to unite with this Church.

2. While I have never made a public confession of Christ, I feel in my heart that I am a Christian. Jesus is my Savior. I FEEL THE NEED OF UNITING WITH THIS CHURCH, and intend to do so.

3. I am a member of another church, but I WILL TRANSFER MY MEMBERSHIP here.

4. I was once a Christian. I WANT TO COME BACK.

5. I AM A CHURCH MEMBER. I feel the need of a fuller consecration, and desire to become more faithful in my Christian duties.

6. I desire to have A TALK WITH THE PASTOR.

NAME ....

ADDRESS ....

The hymnal for the morning service must be a dignified one. For the evening service, if desired, one may use a cheaper and popular book with paper covers. Care must be exercised in the selection of these hymnbooks, however, so that the hymns contained therein, when used, really promote worship and spiritual expression.

X

ASKING FOR MONEY

"Go break to the needy sweet charity's bread,
 For giving is living," the angel said.
"And must I be giving again and again?"
 The peevish and pitiless answer ran.
"Oh, no," said the angel, piercing me through,
"Just give till the Master stops giving to you."
                                    Author unknown.

THE meetings of the Board of Finance (which includes the
Collectors, the Finance Committee, the Treasurers, and the
Pastor) are always moments that test one's spirit. Far too
often this group seems to believe that a minister's success is
determined largely by the results which come from his ability
to strike the hard and flinty rock of conscience and to cause
it to flow forth with gold and silver for the work of the parish
at home and abroad. In this committee, too, every expenditure
which the pastor may have authorized will be submitted to a
cold analysis in the chilling light of retrospect. The members
of this committee are usually the best business men of the
congregation, and as such may be inclined to judge results
merely in the terms of the dollar and cents. They are men
of practical experience, for the most part, and sentiment does
not play too great a part in their attitudes.

Usually they prefer that the pastor should not have too great
a voice in the matter of finances; even though when there is

any falling down in revenues, they are inclined to feel that it is a direct or an indirect result of the pastor's activity or lack of it. And it is a wise pastor who realizes these tendencies, and profits thereby.

The church that has several Treasurers, one in charge of the current fund, one for the building fund, one for the missionary fund, one for the charity fund, and one for the invested funds, is fortunate and far better equipped to meet all of its needs. Responsibility for the entire success of the financial program is thereby diversified, and responsibility does beget interest.

If the pastor were to ask the members of this Finance Committee the pointed question: "What part may I have in carrying the general burden of finance?" he would probably receive the following brief answer: "You may do two things. You may share in the work by your own financial contribution, and you may educate the membership through sermons, conferences and conversations on the matter of adequate parish support."

Often it has served as a check on the pastor's own attitude, if he should ask casually: "What do you expect your pastor to pledge?" Ask it merely to see how one's intention matches with their expectation. Follow up such a question by asking: "Did the former pastor leave unpaid any of his pledges?" If it is at all possible, the new pastor will find it expedient to assume these unpaid obligations.

No discussion of money can be adequate that does not recognize two initial principles: 1. In the acquiring of money there must be always absolute honesty toward God and man; and an absence of the spirit of covetousness. 2. In dispensing money there must be the recognition that all we have belongs to God. We are to be industrious and thrifty, but our frugality and wisdom must never become thorns to choke the wheat of generosity.

In every field of service excepting religion, we pay for what we receive—and we are willing to do it. But in religion we ask for no stipulated sum, no dues are required, only the offering plate is passed, and what goes into it is left to one's conscience. The result is that the Church, the missionary school, the religious school, and the various agencies of the Church institution are continuously handicapped in service. And any general discussion of the subject is regarded as disagreeable and out of place. We are therefore torn between a divided personality—a consciousness of duty and a consciousness of the debts we have assumed. Yet no subject is more important to the individual Christian, for his attitude toward money and its acquisition and its disbursement is usually an indication of his attitudes toward all matters of the Kingdom and to the workaday world. Likewise the Church's attitude toward money is indicative of Its own attitudes. It must have funds like any other result-seeking organization, to carry on Its ever-increasing program of service.

Finances receive treatment from Genesis to Revelation. In Genesis, Abraham gave tithes; in Exodus, Moses commanded his followers not to appear before God with hands empty of an offering; in Deuteronomy, we are reminded that the Lord God gives the power to get wealth; in Joshua, the case of Achan and his lust for gold shows the downfall of a character; in Psalms, we are admonished to appear before God bringing an offering; in Malachi, we are to bring tithes. In Matthew, we are urged to lay up treasure in heaven and not upon earth where thieves break through and steal; and in II Corinthians, we are told that the Lord loveth a cheerful giver. And this is only a partial list.

There are two avenues of approach to finances: there are those who cling to the Old Testament statute of paying the tithe; and there are those who assume the New Testament attitude that our all belongs to God. Paul reminds us in I Corinthians 16:1 and 2, "Let everyone lay by in store upon the first day of the week as God hath prospered him." In other words, he answers the question, When shall we give: his answer is; *Regularly.* When the pay envelope comes in, give to God, first. Remove this matter of giving from emotion and definitely place it in the realm of habit. What sort of a wife would she be who prepared dinner for her husband only when she felt like it!

Paul's answer also makes it possible for the poor to give. Thus the poor person may give ten cents per Sunday, and in a year will have given $5; whereas if he had waited to give the $5 in a lump sum it could never have been done. The shrewdest business men have been the ones who have seen quickly the value of a continual stream of small gifts. Ask Wrigley, the gum vender; Will Hayes, the movie man; Woolworth of the ten cent store organization; or Hearst, the owner of newspapers! These enterprises are now integral parts of human activities: all of them have been predicated upon a large number of small sales.

Who should give? The Apostle says, *"everyone."* Even the widow with the two mites, the boy with the five loaves and two small fishes, the blind French woman who makes her living plaiting straw who gives in the course of a year only 27 francs, which is the price of the oil she saves in her blindness; and from these on up to the merchant princes.

Immanuel Kant says the test of all morality is in answering the question, "Would I be willing for everyone to do as I do?" The person who boasts about benevolence but who scatters and dissipates it and thereby pauperizes society is not a true giver in the Biblical sense. There are, of course, many organizations which have grown up outside the Church and these should have the support of those who are able to give. But these outside causes are to be regarded as an outgrowth of Christian teaching. Had the people in former ages of Christian history observed the principle that Paul lays down, the Church today would have been equipped to enfold all these agencies within Its own activities.

How much should one give? The answer of Paul is *"as one has prospered."* One very poor organization within our city required of everyone in the membership a tithe, and the average per capita giving for the entire congregation last year was $63.92. The average person will pay 90 cents on the dollar to preserve his property, 50% of his income to save his life; but many a man has not yet reached the place where he will pay 10 cents on the dollar to save his soul, or to provide for a continuance of the Christian Church.

Read the story of Barnabas in Acts 4:31-37 and 9:27 and also 11:22 to 30. Even his treatment of the young man John Mark who so irritated Paul becomes a part of the picture. "For he was a good man, and full of the Holy Ghost and of faith." Only when his possessions were disposed of could Barnabas go on a missionary journey.

Another great incentive to giving is suggested by the text found in II Chronicles 29:27: "When the burnt offering began, the song of the Lord began also." Giving may be wedded to ecstatic joy. If you can tell your people when and why, you will have given them enlightenment. When the current budget is over-subscribed, everyone rejoices and forgets the hurt in giving.

Repeatedly raise the question of indirect giving. Tactfully try to say in your sermons and conversations that you do not approve of revenue producing suppers, festivals, bazaars and rummage sales. But "henpecking" is as bad in a pastor as in a wife. Mary Roberts Rinehart defines "henpecking" as telling a smart man more than once!

But do not quote John 2:12-17. Your woman's society respect you highly, and they are working hard for your sake. The husbands of the group are not all generously inclined. There is something to be said for the devotion of these women. One talented woman once quoted Ex. 35:25-35 to me with such vigor that it left me gasping. I still think direct giving the better way.

TRUST FUNDS

Invite the committee on Invested Funds to your home. Such funds grow only by slow and diligent cultivation. One church prepared this card:—

To the COMMITTEE ON TRUST FUNDS:

As an expression of my gratitude to the First Church, and in order that it may continue to work for advancement in knowledge, holiness and service, I hereby subscribe to the Trust Funds the following amount:

* ....

Signature ....

Address ....

Date ....

   * Details concerning payment may be arranged with the committee.

This was sent to a carefully selected list with a memorial statement of the funds then in hand; and of the securities in which they were invested.

A legal form of a will was inserted as a regular item in the weekly calendar, and one day this graph followed the insertion:

THE MAKING OF A CHRISTIAN WILL

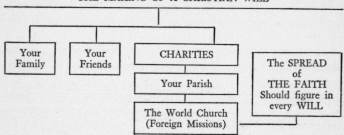

On the Sunday of its appearance the pastor quoted Luke 16:19-31, suggesting: Evil has befallen many Protestant downtown churches. When we see what has happened to famous churches in New York, Chicago, and San Francisco, we wonder if any Protestant church can long survive in a great downtown area unless it has been endowed. The ghosts of these dead churches plead as did Dives (Luke 16:27) that someone will speak to the living and avert disaster for them. Tremont Temple, Park Street Congregational and King's Chapel, all on Beacon Hill in Boston, testify that the downtown church can be saved.

CAMPAIGN FOR THE CURRENT BUDGET

Usually on a day set in the late fall, the pastor is reminded by the chairman of the budget committee that he should have

in preparation the strongest sermon on giving he can preach
—although the average pastor has already had the matter in
mind for weeks and months. Such a sermon is to be part
of the campaign. In the meantime the committee has probably sent out a similar letter to the following:

My dear Fellow-Member:

"Your church is happy, up to date, successful and forward looking." That was said by a wise man who visited us recently. Every person who heard the remark agreed. We believe it is a
general feeling in which you share. Our attendance is good; our
departments are well organized, and our people compose a busy,
happy membership.

Particularly is this true as regards the finances. As the world
judges wealth, we are not a wealthy people, but based upon the
higher concept, we have much of which we may boast, and for
which we may be thankful.

We possess a willing and generous spirit. This has been demonstrated in our giving during the dark days of depression. We
have not failed.

Your committee is going to try an experiment this fall, and are
asking your cooperation. We are going to ask you to take the
envelopes from the collectors at the church on Sunday, November
4, either morning or evening. If we are to raise the budget it will
be necessary for all of us to give as much as last year, and more if
possible each Sunday. This we leave to you. Take your envelope.
Pray about it, and start giving on the first Sunday in January.
Unless you tell us differently, we will hold your pledge as of the
previous year, but we ask you nonetheless to sign the card, if you
will please.

Your committee feels sure that as the Lord has prospered you,
so will you want to make suitable return to Him for the carrying
on of His work locally and throughout the world. If you care to
increase the amount, you will voluntarily do so.

Our goal will be—A regular and suitable contribution from
every member able to contribute.

If we accomplish this, we shall be blessed as we have been in the past. Let us support our church and pastor; take our envelope, and give according to our means.

Thank you.

FINANCE COMMITTEE.

The pastor must be prepared from year to year to respond to this challenge from the Finance Committee. Hence, it will be necessary for him constantly to stock his files full of clippings, stories, facts, unusual slants on financial matters, statistics which can be used to develop a thought, so that they may be used to fortify the "strongest sermon on finances."

Here is one way in which a pastor responded to such a challenge, by preaching on

"A GIFT OF ALABASTER"

> Text: John 12:3—"Then took Mary a pound of ointment of spinkenard very costly and anointed the feet of Jesus and wiped his feet with her hair, and the house was filled with the odor of the ointment."

This incident, or one somewhat similar, is recorded in all four of the gospels. The discrepancies in the accounts are more seeming than real, and I believe can be harmonized or explained. The incident in brief is this: Six days before the crucifixion Jesus came to Bethany and lodged in the house of Simon the Pharisee, who had been a leper before Jesus had healed him. The children of this family—Mary, Martha, and Lazarus—were all deeply devoted to Jesus. While the family were at meat Mary brought out a twelve ounce flask of pure liquid nard or perfume and poured it on Jesus' body. Whether there was one anointing or two, whether it was in the north or the south, and what was the character even, of the woman, has been a matter of deep debate. If you allow that there were two anointings all our troubles of exegesis are solved.

The value of the flask was then about sixty dollars and today would bring perhaps twelve hundred dollars. The poet Horace offers a cask of his costliest wine for such a flask. And Herodotus says that such a vase was one of five gifts sent by Cambyses to the King of Ethiopia, and that its value was that of the wages of a man for a year. The attar of roses made in Ghazipoor in India in which four hundred thousand full grown blossoms go to make one ounce of perfume, which sells for one hundred dollars, is perhaps our nearest modern equivalent to this beautiful ancient gift of devoted love. This flask that she broke was the kind used in anointing the dead. When she broke the flask she wept and kissed his feet and wiped them with her hair. There are in the picture five elements, each demanding thought. There is a needy home; a woman; a carping and dishonest critic; an act of love; and a redeeming cross. Think for a moment of that home. Have you ever considered that there were not many homes where Jesus was so whole-heartedly welcomed. One in Cana, three in Capernaum, one in Jericho, one in Jerusalem, one in Bethany. Just seven such homes in all Palestine!

This act of love, the act of this oriental woman toward our Lord is *arresting* in its quality. It grips our attention. When one of Baltimore's great preachers, Dr. Sparhawk Jones, went to Princeton University to preach and when he was told that attention was difficult to hold at the chapel service, he arose and announced as his text, "Is thy servant a dog that he should do this thing?" Then he said abruptly, "Dog or no dog, he did it." And he had the attention of the students instantly and effectually. This incident is of the same challenging sort. Her heart was speaking its love. Jesus would die within ten days. She did not know that, but He did. Her act to Him took on all the sacrament of burial.

Her act is intensely *melodramatic*. It was typically oriental. It could not happen here for we pride ourselves that we are self-contained. We are ashamed of tears. We do not show our hearts except in the movies. Years ago as a boy I was at the railway station. A farmer's aged wife was taking the train. She was little in stature, grey, and somewhat feeble. With her was her honest, hard-handed, hard-working husband. Visits to town were infrequent. This trip was an event and well it might be. The local doctor had diagnosed her case as malignant. She was going to the State University and to its free operating clinic. The farmer and his four tall sons stood looking down at the little black-bonneted, trembling figure. She might never return alive. The husband rubbed the red plush seat with his palm and said "Goodbye" and stalked out acting almost ashamed. Kindly enquiring eyes were all about; ready hands were there. But he and the boys were too embarrassed for any demonstration of tenderness. They had inherited training in the school of repression. Where they came from there were few words spoken, and few of those when uttered were tender. Even as a boy I had wanted to shout: "Kiss her, you may never have another chance." But not so with the East, for the East is not ashamed to show its heart. The Mohammedan finds no difficulty quite sincerely and self-forgetfully in kneeling in the street to pray at the call of the muezzin, while we would wonder who would see us in such an act and report it with ribald laughter in the club an hour later. There is nothing we are more afraid of here in the Occident than exhibition.

America is growing a set of Spartan virtues. It would permit a fox of pride to gnaw out its vitals rather than show anyone that it deeply cares about anything spiritual, or that it can be deeply moved in the realm of religion.

This woman's act was *memorial*. Jesus said so. It may be well to ask ourselves the question "What kind of a memorial is it?" Memorials are in every park and every cemetery, but often you cannot tell what is memorialized. Is it a remembrance to the dead? or is it a monument to the vanity, wealth, and bad taste of the living? This woman erected a memorial not to the tender kindliness instinctive in every woman's heart, but to her own discovery of the Jesus who forgave her sins.

Midway in Jesus' life, Peter too made a great discovery. He confessed, "Thou art the Christ, the Son of the living God." Thereupon Jesus declared that forever afterward the real Church in all ages would be made up of those who builded their lives upon the rock of faith that Jesus was the anointed Son of God;

and that building our lives upon that Rock will give to our lives the quality of permanency. This was the fact this woman memorialized. Simon, the host of that hour, saw in Jesus a guest to be patronized. The crowd saw in Jesus a celebrity. Judas saw in Jesus a failing fanatic. But this woman alone saw her Savior, the One who had opened for her the way to God and a holy life. Her motive was love, if it is proper in a case like this to look for motives. The sincerest reflexes are never motivated consciously. They are the involuntary expressions of one's deepest nature and as such are to be trusted, provided the nature itself is trustworthy. She loved Jesus, and she gave the gift while he was yet alive. I always have been glad of that. Joseph of Arimathea might give a hundred weight of spices later, but she gave her gift while he was yet alive. I would rather my coffin should be without a single flower, my funeral without a song, my grave without a mourner, and the stone without an epitaph, than to die not having known this sweet joy of self-forgetful love. That was the very essence of her gift.

Her act became therefore both *prophetic and symbolic*. Henceforth the best and sweetest fragrance of her life was to be poured out in wild abandon upon sinning humanity in the service of Jesus. I trust then that my homily shall not be thought far-fetched when I pursue this symbolism for me and my Church. We too have an alabaster box which we may break upon our Lord's head. We see a soldier obey the mandate of his country. The flag waves, the trumpet sounds the call, the army marches away. The zero hour arrives, the charge is given, and by and by they bring the poor broken body back to bury it. The precious ointment of life blood, of a thinking mind, a loving heart, and plans for years ahead, has been poured out on the altar of love for one's country. But shall my country demand a sacrifice from me more costly than that I am willing to give to my Lord! And am I willing to give my life as freely in the service of my Lord?

In the aeroplane, man has mastered land and sea and air. After patient research a motor was invented, a wing spread devised, a purified gas screened and distilled; and now oceans are spanned. Yet this was not done without the breaking of the alabaster box of sacrifice. The earth and sea are stained with blood; and earth's remotest jungle is heavy with the sacrifice of human life.

In this day of modern capitalism, factory smoke darkens every sky. It too asks for its missionaries and martyrs. Go to any steamship dock where men go down to the sea in great ships, and what do you see? Men by the scores bidding goodbye to their families and home comforts for months. For what? That the world may have oil and cigarettes and movies and soap and shoes. They are breaking every sweet-smelling alabaster box of home love —and for what?

But someone says I have no alabaster box. Yes, I have; for anything you possess, whatever it be, which you gladly give to Jesus for His dear sake or for that of the world of men He longs to save becomes an alabaster box to Him. Half of the glory of this gift of the woman lies in the fact that she gave what she had. This is what He is always looking for—the gift you are able to make. In the case of the poor widow—her two mites, her all. And with the rich young ruler, his all.

There is first of all the alabaster box of self. The gift of that woman that day stands out in strange contrast with the gift of Simon. Had he not given much? He had given his time, his thought, and his treasure to an elaborate repast ostensibly to honor a distinguished guest. Surely there is nothing here to object to or to criticize. Why put the relatively small gift of an oriental woman higher in the niche of fame than the lavish gift of Simon? Well, for one reason at least—she gave herself with her gift. And this is the Scriptural measure surely! This they did! They first of all gave themselves unto the Lord.

Have you consciously said to your Lord? "Here am I. O Lord take me." He who would break the alabaster box must begin by making an entire dedication of his life to Jesus regardless of where it may take him and of whatever it may demand. It will, of course, take you into the Church. A life given to Jesus must be related to some organized expression of His will. You might as well attempt to convince a business man that you were devoted to him while giving all your energies to promote a rival organization. Then, too, such a dedication may and quite possibly will take you into the ministry or to the foreign field. It may cause you to give up your most cherished friendships and your dearest plans for your life. All this is conceivable.

But break the flask! Say to the Son of God in the soul expressions of Frances Ridley Havergal:

"Take my life and let it be
    Consecrated, Lord, to Thee;
Take my hands and let them move
    At the impulse of Thy love.
Take my feet and let them be
    Swift and beautiful for Thee;
Take my voice and let me sing
    Always, only, for my King.
Take my will and make it Thine,
    It shall be no longer mine;
Take my heart, it is Thine own,
    It shall be Thy royal throne."

Break also the precious flask of your time. There are too many who, like Ananias, wish to give a part of the gift but who prefer to keep the major part for themselves. The closet of prayer is waiting. The pages of Holy Scripture are awaiting your study. Your Church is awaiting fidelity in your attendance. Some office in the Church is awaiting your act of dedication. It will cost your time. That is a gift I am suggesting. There are people who would be insulted to have a dinner guest keep the feast long waiting, who are habitually late for the hour of worship. Are you a lover? You would be outraged to have your lover forget or delay his tryst. Yet who are we or what hearts are ours who find it so easy to forget or despise a prayer service!

Break also the alabaster box of your money! This gift that represented a small fortune she could give without a thought because she had received his love and forgiveness and had given in return her heart and her tears. It is trite to say money is the easiest and cheapest gift we ever give Jesus. Jesus will have no trouble with the contents of your pocketbook if He can first have you. The test of every Church is not financial, but spiritual. I know a man working nights who has a sick wife and two children. It is a heavy burden. Yet I have never heard him complain about money. He always says, "Never mind, Mary; we're getting on fine. You are going to be well some day." And when he shows me to the door, he smiles and says, "That Mary of mine, she's a wonderful woman." There's the secret. He loves her, and sacrifices are mere incidents in a life that glows with love. "I'd do anything for Mary and the kids!" is his constant assurance.

If you do not love Jesus, the trustees of the Church will never be able to break the alabaster box with a sledge hammer. If they do break it, the contents will be so hard that they will not flow.

And may I further suggest that you break the alabaster box of your personal work. Try this year to win at least one soul to Jesus Christ and to His Church. This is probably the most difficult gift that Christ asks from the Church of today. There is no place where greater thought and tact must be shown. But if the readiness first be there God will help.

There are many other things in your life I make no doubt that the alabaster box may represent. In the case of Little Dorrit it was only a smile, but Charles Dickens says it was "a smile straight out of heaven."

When a week after this incident Mary saw her Lord's body broken by thorns and by nails and spear, and saw through those gaping rents in the vase His life blood flowing, I am sure she understood His words which until then had been puzzling to her: "Against the day of my burying hath she done this." I feel sure she never regretted her act. In comparison with His sacrifice how small her own now appeared.

Let us hear our Lord speaking to us today.

> "I gave my life for thee,
>   My precious blood I shed,
> That thou might ransomed be,
>   And quickened from the dead.
> I gave, I gave my all for thee;
>   What hast thou given for me?"

Each year some new plan for handling the subscription cards must be devised for solicitation. A chest shaped like the ark of the covenant may be employed for several years. The entire membership marches by and deposits the cards. After the third Sunday the small remaining list of non-subscribers are visited by the canvassing committee.

Another year the pledge cards may be laid on an open Bible, and the following year a cross may be erected above a cairn of stones and people may be asked to come and deposit their pledge cards at the foot of the cross. A certain few may have been spoken to, a child of three, an older child, a youth, an aged mother, a prominent church official of great means, several of the foreign speaking group, representatives of various organizations who can be coached to say "I come for the Dorcas Class, etc." A group of girls in white who come singing, "Take my life and let it be," may be impressive.

A good many years ago I took some notes of an address given by a prominent religious leader, in which he made the following comments on raising money for religious enterprises. He indicated in this address, which I trust I have reported faithfully, that he recognized seventeen important considerations which every pastor and religious worker must face up to in the raising of funds:

1. You must have a cause which you thoroughly believe in, so that what you say indicates a definite conviction.

2. You must say enough to make your case, and present it so clearly that those who hear you are convinced of the merit of the cause and the reasonableness of the method to be employed.

3. Wherever possible, use the face-to-face solicitation method. Do not write a letter when it is possible to have

a personal interview. By using the face-to-face solicitation method, you make an interested friend for your cause, instead of only a contributor. Your own personality becomes related to the gift and giver, and interest is sustained.

4. Cultivate the habit of looking continuously for leads, not on the basis of how much can I get out of him, but how can his power, his interest, his influence be related to the causes of the Kingdom of God.

5. Work for larger gifts. Translate your opportunities and interests into larger gifts.

6. Never despise a small gift. As a rule, the smaller gifts carry with them more personal interest and prayer.

7. Seek to increase by enlisting continuous interest. Keep in touch with each prospect or contributor not for the sake of receiving a contribution from him, but for keeping him in more vital touch with the work you represent.

8. Cultivate the partnership idea.

9. Make wise and careful use of printed material. Think of the other man's interest, and send him only such printed material as may help to relate his interest to that of your own.

10. Use personalities to help you. Wherever possible secure some influential person in the community to help you by accompanying you.

11. Appeal for specific objects wherever possible. Vagueness usually results in negative reactions.

12. Do not spend the money before you have it. It is easier to raise money to carry forward a work than to appeal for funds to settle a deficit.

13. Put a time limit on yourself. Do not procrastinate. Many opportunities have been lost because one waited too long before presenting a cause.

14. Use the momentum of success.

15. Regard the matter of finances as you would do soul-winning. The elements of personality, will, immediacy and God are all involved.

16. Emphasize always the spiritual side of giving. You are not primarily interested in their gifts; you are interested in the spiritual blessings which will come to them as an indirect result of sharing in the work.

17. Make the whole question a matter of very earnest prayer. God can open the hearts of men and women far more effectively than you can ever do without His Help.

Last summer I visited Yosemite National Park, conducting the Sunday service at Wauwona Inn, in collaboration with my son. We came in from Sacramento by automobile. We visited Placerville, and saw the monument to James W. Marshall who discovered gold and started the rush of 1849. We went on to Lake Tahoe and looked down upon it from a height of a thousand feet or more, reveling in its riot of color, cobalt and azure, indigo and nile green. Here we dropped down the dirt mountain road by eight switchbacks into Minden, Nevada, then on through Bridgeport with its Indian population and up over what seemed to me the dangerous but highly scenic, and never to be forgotten Tioga Pass, coming in the back way of the park, at a height of more than nine thousand feet. It seemed as I gloried in all this grandeur as if God one bright morning might have said, "Go to, now, I am going to produce one perfect piece of work in nature that all may know me at my best." We came down over the Control Road where cars are allowed to go in but one direction up or down each alternate hour. We marvelled at the precision with which the rangers keep track of all cars and all entrants so that it is probable that of the three hundred thousand who enter in a single season the United States government could tell approximately your location at almost any moment of your stay. As we rounded the turn El Capitan, the great grey giant, raised its head. God had carved it, a perfect jewel. Underneath its sombre grey shone just a faint suggestion of pink which may have belonged to the stone or to the evening hour. Across the valley the Bridal Veil was softly floating in the breeze. Below us lay the valley floor. Before evening we had hiked to the Yosemite Falls, three precipitous bits of glory, fourteen hundred, nine hundred, and three hundred feet, each cascading after the other in quick succession. In the morning we visited the Mariposa grove of big trees, the *Sequoia Gigantea*. We drove to Inspiration Point, and allowed our eye to take in the entire panorama, these wonders we had already seen, and Half Dome, and Sunset Peak, and Clouds Rest, and Cathedral Peaks. I lifted my voice and sang, what another had taught me:

> "The hills of God uphold the skies
> Let heavenly hallelujahs rise.
> Let rocks and hills and heavenly host,
> Praise Father, Son, and Holy Ghost."

It is the only Doxology for Yosemite!

We had quickly located the points of outstanding greatness in the Park,—El Capitan, The Falls, the Trees, the Panorama—but that night we were to have the delirious joy of seeing the greatest sight of all, the Fire Fall. I had read of it a dozen times but nothing I had read had prepared me for the beauty that I saw. A vast concourse of people had begun to gather at every vantage point in the Park shortly after sunset. A musical program had been prepared of outstanding excellence by imported artists, for those more advantageously located. The men who prepare the fire start it at about six P.M. The embers are produced by an especially chosen fuel perhaps especially treated, I do not know. Promptly at nine o'clock the concert stops, the huge throng stands and turns expectantly toward the towering cliff of scarped rock rising a half mile at least toward the sky. The leader of the orchestra raises his voice and calls in a shout that is almost a song, "Are you ready?" After perhaps a half a minute of perfect silence comes the answer from above the abyss, "We are ready." Again our leader shouted, "Then let the fire fall." And from above, "Let the fire fall."

It came as a trickle, then a shimmering stream, then a cataract. It continued to fall steadily for perhaps ten minutes. It looked not like brands of coal, or embers even, but like a river, a Niagara of ruby splendor. Its color was soft blue, purple, and rose. There was no harsh look of burning flame. This was not fire to hurt, or to sear, or to scorch, or to consume. This was the warm glow of jewels, the soft velvet of the morning glory, the promise of dawn in the eastern sky. The sensual notes of "Liebestraum" that the pianist before had been playing were hushed and now the soloist was singing, "I Know That My Redeemer Liveth"—"I know—Yes I know—and because He lives I *too*—I *too*—I *too* shall live!"

This was more than a spectacle. It was a profound spiritual experience. God was entering our hearts. He was whispering with deep enticement, "Let the fire fall! Open your heart my child to what I would send you from heaven."

Suddenly I had one of those telepathic bits of insight in

which I knew what Jesus had meant when he parted from his disciples. "Tarry ye in Jerusalem until ye be endued with power from on high." I saw that early church no longer "with doors shut for fear of the Jews," but now "all together in one place," praying, thinking, counseling, surrendering their hearts. Then suddenly an uprush and release of the Spirit's power takes place, and the Crucified Christ has His chance. Fear is gone. Certainty has come. Half-considered, half-concealed truths become plain. Individuals lose their identity, and a great movement has been born. An organization has come into being, not of design but of necessity. A message has crystallized. Jesus is the World's Savior. The cross is the necessary path of revelation and redemption. There is no life now possible for each one of them save to tell the story. They must give their all. "Jesus Christ whom ye crucified hath God raised from the dead. . . . . . . And in none other is there salvation. For there is none other name under heaven, given among men whereby ye must be saved." Why hadn't they seen this so realistically before? May we mediate such an experience to our congregation; when we do, giving becomes easy.

When we ministers receive "fire from heaven," we shall never have to look for "convincing arguments" for giving to the work of the Christian Church.

May such an experience be ours!

XI

THE SHEPHERD OF THE FLOCK

My FATHER, like so many of his generation, was a strict sabbatarian. On one Sunday in my childhood, I remember, my father was returning with us from the worship service. On the way home he noticed on a railroad siding a double-deck cattle car loaded with sheep and lambs. They had evidently been shipped a long way, and did not arrive in time to be unloaded before the Sabbath; so since the transportation companies those days provided no care on Sunday for animals in transit, they were forced to stay there unattended and uncared for until the Sabbath was over.

As my father, forced by his compassion for animals in distress, stopped, he noticed that one of the small lambs had fallen, and was in danger of being stepped on. He had no financial interest in the animals, and was under no obligation to care for them. But I do remember seeing my father break the Old Testament law of the Sabbath in a manner that my own upbringing at that time could not account for, for he spent that afternoon trying to rescue that lamb and caring for those unfortunate animals.

This memory of my father and the little lamb is a vivid one. All these years it has served to show me the relationship between the sheep in the railroad car and those whom Jesus designated in his command: "Feed my sheep." And I see a parallel between my father and my Heavenly Father, Whose compassion knows no limitations.

Those of us of the older generation, of course, remember many similar experiences with sheep. We recall the cruel method which was employed then by which the sheep were plunged into the icy waters in the early spring, preparatory to the shearing. We recall vividly the small and larger flocks of sheep taken from one pasture to another over the dusty, country roads, inhaling the choking dust and pushing one another in confusion. And we recall far too well the dirty, ill-smelling place where the animals were slaughtered—a sight which even wilted a boy's heart.

We recall with pleasure the salting of the sheep. One stood at the pasture gate with a huge burlap bag filled with coarse salt and threw salt in quantities upon the ground, calling softly "cŏ-dā′!" And when the sheep heard that call, they came on the run. The shepherd dog was there, too, wise beyond belief, watching to see that no stray was left far behind.

But in the passing of the years all of this has changed, until today the Twenty-third Psalm is recited on Sunday with perhaps only a little meaning, while on Monday the voice over the telephone orders, a rib chop, a rolled shoulder, or a five and a half pound roast, adding "and please send me a can of peas, and a bottle of mint sauce."

Yet, in the days of the Old Testament and the New the name shepherd had great significance. The occupation carried with it great loyalty, a love for the sheep, and an inborn feeling of responsibility.

It is that concept of the shepherd that I wish to carry over for the thought of the discussion in this important chapter. For a pastor is truly the shepherd of a flock. Pastoral theology is often called poimenics, from the Greek word poimen'—a sheep. The word has been used for so long a time that we do not realize that it is a figure of speech, a metaphor. It was already in familiar use in Jeremiah's day.*

A pastor is a shepherd; or rather, the duties of a shepherd are his duties; feeding sheep; tending lambs, their care and nurture. The dangers of a shepherd are his dangers, loneliness, hunger, cold, exposure to weather and wild beasts. The rewards of a shepherd are his rewards, the affection of the flock and a meagre subsistence from this livelihood. But the figure cannot tell it all. We labor under a Great, a Good, a Chief Shepherd.** Our expectation of reward is from Him.

A congregation is a flock. Sometimes a troublesome one. "All we like sheep have gone astray." (Isa. 53:6.) Discontented, nomadic, blind to obvious danger, easily stampeded.

Let those boast who will of the fisherman's ring, bestowed upon Peter. That was early in his discipleship. Remember though that the last word of Jesus spoken to Peter was "Feed my sheep"; and consequently our real badge of office is the shepherd's crook. Ours is not the mitre and crozier, but the more humble shepherd's cap and rod or staff with its crook, from which the more glorious symbols later sprung.

There is no designation of our calling so important, so endearing as "Pastor." Not rector, ruler; nor Dominie, master; nor parson, person; nor elder, oldster; nor preacher, herald; nor prophet, stern speaker for God; nor priest, mediator; but pastor, shepherd—the one who feeds and finds and fends and folds the flock.

To be sure, there are functions of effective service to perform

---

* Jer. 2:8; 3:15; 10:21; 12:10; 17:16; 22:22; 23:1-2.
** John 10:14; Heb. 13:20; 1 Pet. 5:4.

other than shepherding. Apostles, prophets, evangelists, teachers, each have importance. There is no first nor last. But we are shepherds.

THE PASTOR LEADS HIS FLOCK—SOFTLY

One has not read far into that old book, whose pages are as yellow as gold and much more precious, before he comes upon the story of the perfect shepherd. Here is Jacob. (Gen. 33: 14.) Doomed to be a wanderer and an itinerant like many of us; his wages often changed, by an overlord who should have known sympathy and didn't; wringing success out of the hard hand of failure, out of sheer love; finally, resigning from his field and stealing away with forlorn heart praying that God will not let him down, but would help him to open up some new field. The story of Jacob is always so autobiographical. And so here in the Scripture account is Jacob praying all night, with mighty wrestlings, "I will not let Thee go except Thou bless me." That is Jacob's garden of prayer. Watch him the next day, when prayer has done its work. Self is forgotten, and he thinks of the women and the children and the flock.

"My lord knoweth that the children are tender and the flocks and herds with young are with me; and if men should overdrive them one day, all the flock will die. . . . I will lead on softly . . . as the cattle and the children be able to endure."

And so the pastor too must be a considerate leader. "He goeth before them, and the sheep follow him: for they know his voice." (John 10:4.) Therefore, he must know the path himself, for he sets the pace. He does not consult the most influential financial bell-wether of the flock, nor lay out the path according to the dictates of an independent ram.

Likewise, the pastor must lead in giving, in prayer, in morality, in humility, in love and in foresight. He must seek ever to lead his men in their own activities, and be a true shepherd to them.

He must seek to lead his women, too, for the women's society has become established and accepted everywhere. Every woman in the Church is there by virtue of her membership. I Corinthians 14:34 must be matched with Galatians 3:28.

Women accompanied Jesus on His errands of mercy. (Luke 8:3.) There is evidence that Paul employed women as deaconesses in spite of his directions about women keeping silent in the churches. (Rom. 16:1.) The Roman Catholic Church makes use of this passion in woman's heart for service to the Lord, by making them nuns or sisters in various orders of the Church, receiving from them the vow of poverty, chastity and obedience.

Protestant Churches have both scriptural sanction * and historical usage and the counsels of good sense in the creation of deaconesses and pastor's assistants.

To the Deaconesses may be entrusted the visitation of the sick; the instruction and care of candidates; the preparation and care of the Table with its linen, its vessels and its emblems. They should perform much of the instruction in the religious school and exercise the care of much of the church charity, and the promotion of goodwill.

The tenure of office for the Chairman of the Board of Deaconesses should be one year. The term of office for members of the board should be three years with an enforced intermission of one year before eligibility to reelection.

There should also be a board of Junior Deaconesses. The

---

* Rom. 16:6; Acts 1:14; 16:1-15; 6:1; 18:26; I Tim. 3:11; Phil. 4:2-3.

purpose of such a group is to serve as understudies, receiving training for eligibility.

THE WOMAN'S SOCIETY

The woman's society should, if possible, unite in one organization all functions, not forgetting the study of missions and the promotion of church contributions. Christianity is declared in Acts 10: and 15: to be universal in character. Christians owe a debt to all lands. The Church has expanded to every nation. The present decline which is alarming in missionary gifts can only be met by information, organization and development. This should be one of the major tasks of a woman's society.

The woman's society should have a welcoming committee at the door; should have a nursery during the morning worship to which young mothers may take their babies up to five years of age; should care for all vestments; should appoint the floral committee; and should keep in close touch with parish visitation.

They will serve on the missionary committee of the church; promote the reading contests; maintain missionary instruction in the school; provide a scholarship in the Training School; supervise the budget; do White Cross work, making layettes for mission stations; and carry forward other definite projects.

They may conduct classes in Americanization among the foreign born, and promote the Sewing school and the Mothers' club.

The pastor, as leader, will lighten his labors if he makes leaders of them.

YOUTH IN THE CHURCH

The place of youth in the Christian Church is clearly indicated in Acts 2:17 and I John 2:14. In 1844 George Williams founded the Y.M.C.A., and in 1881 in Portland, Maine, was born the Christian Endeavor Society, fostered by Dr. Francis E. Clark. The Student Volunteer Movement for Foreign Missions came into being through the combined consecration and efforts of Robert P. Wilder, John R. Mott, Robert Forman, Robert E. Speer, Sherwood Eddy, and other "Student Volunteers" whose influence has left its stamp upon the missionary program of the American Christian Church, as they adopted as their watchword: "The evangelization of the world in this generation."

But even today the latent power in the youth of every church is like the waters of Niagara, 99% of which goes over the falls in reckless volume and in glorious display, and only 1% of which finds its way into the turbines whereby energy is transformed into electric power.

Fortunate the pastor who can harness some of this youth power. Once a year the pastor will ask his youth (18 to 25 years) to take over the entire morning service. They provide the choir and take over every detail, including the sermon.

Monthly Firesides should be held for these groups in suitable homes after the evening service. Here, popular singing will be encouraged. It should be spontaneous. It cannot be repressed but it may be guided. From the ephemeral, it may be led into "Are ye able," and other great hymns. An abundance of popular musical material exists of a devout character.*

---

* Singing Worship by Edith L. Thomas, Abingdon Press, is excellent for this purpose.

A meeting may be held during the Christmas vacation for students returned from the colleges. Another service for all graduates of high schools and colleges will be held in June before the summer vacation exodus has taken place. Here again the youth will provide almost the entire program.

To secure the complete list a paper will be posted in the foyer and every graduate will be asked to sign his own name, there. Otherwise awkward omissions sometimes occur. The congregation will be glad to cooperate in making the list complete.

Usually some gifted youth may be found who will provide weekly posters for the young people's service.

Youth activities of a social nature will include play parties for mutual acquaintance, hikes, excursions, basketball games, and the like. Once a year there will be a youth banquet with an outstanding speaker to challenge them to life work, to education or to moral reform. Money should be provided to send some of the more promising youths to summer conferences; in which case the church should never pay more than one-half the entire expense, that is, not to exceed fifteen dollars per person for a two-week period.

THE PASTOR FEEDS HIS SHEEP—WISELY

My wife's family have a story of her childhood that always awakens interested merriment. The spring when she was nine—as the dams were proudly bringing up their lambs to the yard, her father discovered that one dam was missing, perhaps, dead. Poor motherless lamb! What should be done? He put the lambkin in the care of his little daughter. Her maternal instinct would do the rest.

"Be good to it; but not too good. Remember!"

And so she fed it milk from a nippled bottle, and day by day the old story was reenacted: "And everywhere that Mary went, The lamb was sure to go."

But there came a day when the lamb, almost grown, could no longer gambol. It stood, swaying from side to side, or at most hobbling along rather helplessly. And finally it lay down and died.

Then there was much wailing: "What made my lamb die?"

"Well, dear, if you must know; you were too good to it. You fed it too much. You didn't give it enough exercise. The lamb died from gluttony." Fortunate the pastor who learns early in his ministry how to feed the sheep.

> "The hungry sheep look up and are not fed,
> But swoln with wind and rank mist they draw,
> Rot inwardly and foul contagion spread,
> Besides what the grim wolf with privy paw
> Daily devours apace and nothing sed."
> —*Lycidas II: 125-129.*

Over against Milton's stark picture behold another.

On the right wall of the sanctuary of the Congregational Church of Northampton, Massachusetts, there is a bronze plaque to the memory of its greatest pastor:

> In Memory of
> JONATHAN EDWARDS
> MINISTER OF NORTHAMPTON
> *From February 15, 1727 to June 22, 1750*
> *The law of truth was in his mouth and*
> *Unrighteousness was not found in his lips*
> *He walked with me in peace and uprightness*
> *And did turn many away from iniquity.*
> *Mal. 2-6*

There will be no excuse for failure to prepare and deliver a good sermon. The diet will be varied; grass and open pasture in season, grain or millet occasionally. Dry feed, placed low in the rack when winter comes. Not too high! Jesus never said, "Feed my giraffes."

Sermons that edify the saints in the morning. Expositions of scripture, too long neglected. Disclosures of doctrine, too long frowned upon, to our hurt. Daring challenges to missionary enterprise, just now quite out of style. Fearless denunciation of national apostasy, or personal and social immorality as fatal as the black plague.

Nathan, with long finger pointing with faithfulness at a wayward King, and saying, "Thou art the man."

At night, always a popular evening service, that never yields to the cry of the populace but faithfully proclaims to sinners a saving God.

"Green pastures and still waters." Good feeding ground. But not too good! I have seen a congregation with a poor preacher thrive, when he was a diligent and loving shepherd. I never saw the reverse.

A church may too easily become a congregation of "sermon-addicts," who feel that their entire duty to God and man is to attend a morning service and say as they pass down the foyer, "Pastor, what a lovely sermon." No feeding process is complete that does not end in exercise. "He leadeth them forth."

In the process of feeding, children come first. Midway between the Roman Catholic policy of baptizing babies and confirming them later after instruction in classes, and the policy of those Churches that baptize adults and these only after they have felt a Pauline catastrophic experience, there has grown up another group influenced by Dr. Horace Bushnell of Hartford, Conn., (1841). This group makes increasing use of the Bible School and Decision Day. With Paul (Rom. 12:2) they feel that the transformation of life into Christ's likeness may come through the mind and so reach the heart, (John 3:3).

But the instruction of the mind must be good instruction. She came from the class reciting the creed "suffered unconscious piety." That's what she thought they said when they intoned "suffered under Pontius Pilate," and no one had corrected her.

Early in the autumn a service must be held with those teachers in the school who are in the Junior Department and above, clearly setting forth the pastor's desire that every boy and girl above the ninth year should be brought to Christ and into the Church by the following Easter. Questions of method will be answered. The homes must be entered in the fall and cooperation of parents secured thus early.

"What would you think of a boy who kept an *apple* until it was spoiled before he tried to eat it? What would you think of a girl who kept a *rose* until it wilted and faded before she tried to wear it? What would you think of a man who bought an automobile and never used it until it rusted? What would you think of boys and girls who waited until they were men and women before giving their hearts to the Lord Jesus? We are never too young to love Him, and boys and girls should learn to love Jesus just as sweetly and just as surely and just as early as they learn to love their own fathers and mothers in their own homes."

Here is an approach for Decision day. Or the simple recital of Jesus' entry into Jerusalem (Matt. 21:15). "Is your shout heard, too?" Or the story of Tannhauser: He heard the Pilgrim's Chorus on its way to forgiveness. He intended to join them. But the music died away in the distance, and still he did not rise.

Decisions should be registered two weeks before Easter. Baptisms of children are best on Palm Sunday.

Seven weeks before Easter start the pastor's class, on Friday afternoon, after school. The first lesson may be on the life of Christ. A quick survey, Birth, Childhood, Baptism, Temptation, Disciples, Healing, Teaching, The last week, The last Supper, The Betrayal, The Trial, Pilate, The Cross, The Resurrection.

The second lesson will be on man's sin and forgiveness—a quick story of Bunyan's Pilgrim. Possibly a little drill on the Ten Commandments.

The third lesson will be on the Cross and The Seven Last Words.

The fourth lesson is on the Church; the fifth is on Baptism, explaining in detail everything that is done at every step from the moment one appears before the membership committee to the receiving of the Right Hand of Christian Fellowship.

The sixth lesson is on the Lord's Supper. The seventh and last lesson carefully goes over Repentance, Faith and Confession. Then the opportunity for Decision is given.

For hand work in these classes, the pupils may construct a book. The leader will provide the bright colored cover of heavy paper, $8\frac{1}{2}'' \times 11''$. Any stationer can supply "construction paper" or "cover paper" with a vellum finish. These come in packages of fifty, and retail for not to exceed seventy-five cents. When this is folded the booklet becomes $8\frac{1}{2}'' \times 5\frac{1}{2}''$ in size.

Perry pictures or their equivalent in color may be provided

of "Peter and John on the way to the Tomb," of Holman Hunt's "Light of the World," of Leonardo di Vinci's "The Last Supper," of Hofman's "The Rich Young Ruler" or "The Boy Christ in the Temple," or of Watt's "Sir Galahad." In addition to these in penny size, one will carefully mimeograph the typewritten material of these lessons for each child.

I have before me the work sheet of one child on "A good Church Member."

Here are the answers he had worked out for himself.

"A good church member."

1. Hates sin. 2. Loves Christ. 3. Is baptized. 4. Attends worship. 5. Works at something in the church. 6. Gives. 7. Knows his Bible. 8. Tries to win others. 9. Is friendly to other churches. 10. Serves the world by trying to stop war and hunger, and liquor and gambling. 11. Keeps the pastor's office informed about changes of address.

Work for children includes much else. Dedication, construction of a cradle roll (Birth to three years), calling in hospital and home, knowing the child, work in the Sunday School, the Children's sermon, the Children's choir, the Daily Vacation Bible School, and Children's Day.

There is no surer way to give offence to a child than a failure to know his name. "I am Ernest. My brother is Alfred. You tell the folks of the church you love them. But you don't know us apart."

This is not a good recipe for church membership.

The feeding process concerns the church school. For one reason because 85% of the entire yearly accession to a church comes from this source. This theme deserves an entire book. But certain things concerning the school must be said.

1. The school will be *graded*. The Cradle roll, Birth to three

years; Beginners, 4-5; Primary, 6-8; Junior, 9-11; Junior High, 12-15; Senior, 16-17; Senior High, 18-25; Adult, over 25. In addition, there must be a Home Department.

2. The time of meeting will depend on the customs of the locality. Probably more people will attend at 12 o'clock than at nine o'clock, for the earlier hour seems to shut out the attendance of many mothers. But the earlier hour has able advocates.

3. The place of The International lessons is being filled by the excellence of the graded material.

4. Shall the Pastor teach? Theoretically he should be free to visit all Departments. But practically, no pastor can be spared from the list of teachers.

5. Should the entire school meet together for opening worship? It is better to meet by Departments if the building will permit except on a few days such as Rally Day and Promotion Day.

6. The Sunday School Council is composed of all teachers and officers and must meet monthly to consider better teaching methods and should be addressed by an able speaker.

The function of the Board of Education is different from that of the Sunday School Council for it has to do with the management of business pertaining to the Christian Endeavor, the Sunday School, the Boy Scouts, the World Wide Guild, the School of Missions, the Firesides, the Summer Conferences, and the Daily Vacation School.

The Board of Education elects the Superintendent of the Sunday School, and confirms the appointment of all teachers.

THE SHEPHERD FENDS HIS FLOCK—FEARLESSLY

What a story that is of David in First Samuel (17) "And David went . . . to feed his father's sheep at Bethlehem . . . and Eliab his eldest brother . . . spake . . . with whom hast thou left those few sheep in the wilderness? I know thy pride . . . And David said to Saul, Thy servant kept his father's sheep and there came a lion and a bear, and took a lamb out of the flock: and I went out after him and smote him, and delivered it out of his mouth: and when he arose against me, I caught him by his beard . . . and slew him."

Courage! But no more than the modern shepherd will need in meeting the lions and the bears that invade every feeding ground. And an occasional serpent too.

David was all alone. David was in a tight spot. No big brother was near. The situation took all he had. Let no pastor think that such situations do not arise. They are sufficiently frequent so that every pastor recognizes them.

One's flock or some lamb in it is imperilled by strong forces of evil. There is point to the story of the boy at the circus who listened to the barker shouting, "See the lion and the lamb lie down together." He paid his dime and there they were lying pleasantly side by side. When the exhibition was over he asked, "How is it done?"

"Well I'll tell you, farmer, we have occasionally to replenish the lamb." The remorseless recruiting of youth for bar-maids and brothels goes on before our eyes.

These forces must be faced and overcome and the person saved for God. This is what Jesus meant, "Behold I send you forth as sheep in the midst of wolves." (Matthew 10.)

No amount of imagination can prepare us for the unforeseen forces who would fashion our cross. But they are there! Liquor, gambling, lust, drugs. And false doctrine, in myriad forms. And war, racialism, nationalism, and economic wrong.

The lions and the bears stalk the flock, and us. "If they have called the master of the house, Beelzebub how much more they of his household."

But we must not let David's story beguile us. Lions and bears are to be slain. But the weapons of our warfare are not carnal. (II Cor. 10:4.) We stand to proclaim the ceaseless purity of a Holy God. We do not weep in public, over our wounds or scars. And we do not flee. "The hireling fleeth because he is a hireling."

The true shepherd is too busy at his job of saving the flock in peril, to think of flight. And if he thinks of himself at all, he rejoices as a good soldier, and whispers, "standeth God within the shadows, keeping watch above his own."

In the business of shepherding it is almost impossible at times to avoid self pity, or the dramatization of one's conflict. The meanest devil out of hell is the imp called "Self-pity." At times when one's feet tread this valley which Bunyan vividly describes and hears Apollyon whispering in his ear, while perched on Christian's shoulder, one might ask himself, "Why did you enlist in this warfare, if you expected no wounds?"

When I get weak-kneed I read again my boy's copy of *The Three Musketeers* and some valiant pages in Stevenson or Bunyan or Fox' *Book of Martyrs* or even *The Gay Adventures of Robin Hood*. We will be saved much humiliation if we remember that we are not called to easy lives but to save God's sheep. We would better save our pity and our praise for them. For "The good shepherd giveth his life for the sheep."

THE CARE OF THE SICK

One of the most constant duties of the pastor is to minister in great personal danger to the very ill, the aged, the dying. He calls on those who are unable to get out over long periods; he visits the enciente and encouched mother.

If he cannot call, he will telephone. His call must not sound professional, but it must be personal, brief, and bespeak hopefulness.

There is a helpful prayer in the book that he may pray with them, or for them. "Oh, Lord Jesus Christ, who by Thy cross and precious blood hath redeemed us, save us and help us, we humbly beseech thee, Oh Lord! Amen." Brief, but in many cases just enough.

One must ever create without seeming to, the will to live. Always treat the physician fairly. And whenever consulted on confidential matters, remember always to respect confidences.

His most constant reminder should be "I will come any hour of the day or the night should you need me."

At the hospital one always enquires at the desk first. One is never turned away when it is known that he is performing the shepherd's function. But this privilege must not be abused.

Pray for your people by name. Tell them so. Let them see the vest pocket record in which is their name and the hour (9 a.m.) of your accustomed supplication.

Occasionally one will be asked "Will I live?" Life is always in God's hands. One never knows. One is safe in saying, "I hope so. I believe so. That is why you and I are praying together, isn't it? Trust God."

One must not shrink from visiting infectious cases. "They

shall take up serpents and if they shall drink any deadly thing it shall not hurt them." (Mark 16:18.)

But, the gospel does not counsel imprudence. (Matt. 4:6-7.)

THE POOR

The poor seem to have been the constant concern of all the writers of Holy Scripture. (Luke 6:20; 4:18; Mark 14:7; James 2:5; Proverbs 19:17.)

It was the charity of the apostolic church that gave us the story of Ananias. It was Paul's concern for the poor believers in Jerusalem that gave us his loftiest teaching in regard to Christian giving. Christian charity as a function has somewhat decayed as the state has assumed this ministry; and as insurance has become a commonplace. State Charity today provides institutional relief for the orphan and the defective. Lodges, Labor Unions, and many outside agencies provide institutionalized relief for their own.

Denominations have established retirement systems for their clergy. And a thousand private charities, Social welfare groups, and Community Chests are continually carried on. The Florence Crittenton League for unmarried mothers is a case in point.

The care of the poor even yet under the latest social security legislation, is not fully or adequately done by the state, or outside or private relief.

"The poor ye have always with you."

Nor have all our social agencies devoted to philanthropy scratched the surface. Ask the Salvation Army.

Yet we must make the effort. Christmas and Thanksgiving charity in food is a beginning. The Fellowship offering taken at every communion furnishes a small amount to serve direst need of food, fuel, and clothing. This will be administered with absolute secrecy except for a careful audit, and a limitation of the amount available to any family. The church, if possible, should endow a hospital bed, and own a lot in the cemetery.

THE CONFESSIONAL

The shepherd like the physician, breathes the air of contagion. Without divine help he yields to what he absolves in another. Without prayer he may make sin appear less than monstrous in his desire to forgive.

Thomas Binney sensed our need when he wrote:

"Eternal light! Eternal light!
How pure the soul must be,
When, placed within Thy searching sight,
It shrinks not, but with calm delight,
Can live and look on Thee."

One must hear every weakness without surprise. There are sins to which only God is fit to listen. Only the constant application of Divine asepsis will keep one. No half baked view of sin, and no blurred vision of God's holiness will avail. The perfect shepherd must love men like God—that is, until He could die for the shame of it; and hate sin like God—that is, until He feels it driving the nails, to be able to listen, and pity and pray and pardon. It is well to keep a circumstantial record of some of this. But it must be kept inviolate, under lock and key, and perhaps in code.

The most helpful discovery I have ever made in the confessional is to keep the mind of the confessor away from the sin and direct it to the holiness, the majesty and the goodness of

God. Even in a prayer of confession, it is better to adore. Confession may act as a magnet to attract the imagination. The behaviorists are right in the assertion that anything which breaks the muscular routine of habit is in the suppliant's favor. All sin has in it the divided self of the schizophreniac. Our duty is to help them to choose which self to live with, for permanent satisfaction. In their repentance lies their answer. It is of the nature of sin that we do not wish to live with it permanently. Only God can bear eternity. We can bear it too only when we become like Him.

THE FALSE SHEPHERD FLEES—SHAMELESSLY

Both the Old and New Testament alike come sternly to a consideration of the shepherd's character, and to a denunciation of false shepherds.

"Men that know not God or the law," "rebellious and walking in ways that do not profit."

Surely, one may read these words quite realistically, and not do as those who read the medical almanac and think themselves possessed of all the diseases. Let us not too quickly accuse ourselves. But the words will make us thoroughgoing. (Ezekiel 34:2, 8, 10) "The shepherds do not feed the flock." "They have muddied the clear streams where the sheep drink."

Imagine a pastor who is interested in the flock only so long as it can be sheared for its fleece, skinned for its pelt, or fattened for a profitable market.

Imagine a shepherd called rapidly from flock to flock because there was money in it. What a comment on any economic system, in which this is either desirable or possible; or a comment on the man himself or a restive congregation.

But one cannot think of the hireling without envisioning the man who has never learned cooperation.

Competition is never so destructive as in the Church. The basis of cooperation between denominations is self-respect and common decency. The prayer of Jesus "that they all may be one" will be answered. And it will not come by all churches adopting the same program as my church, either. But it will come by a purging of hearts of self-will and pride and by a better informed understanding.

Cooperation may be achieved sometimes by united services celebrating some event which we hold in common. It should be possible to avoid competitive advertising. If the community is canvassed, perhaps there could be an agreement on the allocation of districts to be cultivated.

All work of the Church today is difficult. It is made more so by the termites, white ants and borers that attack our organization. The Sunday paper, the radio, the automobile, the movie, the prevalent low concept of the Christian Sabbath, the competitive commercial spirit that leaves us panting and exhausted on Saturday night, and gives many no time for personal affairs except on Sunday, the Sunday sports program, to name but a few. (Matt. 24:11-22.)

It would seem that churches might at least unite to oppose the open saloon on Sunday, and advocate upholding the sanctity of law.

St. Paul calls the church an organism, a body, with parts and functions, an eye, an ear, a hand and a head who is Christ. What a day that will be when all the churches in an area are the organ of Christ in that area to bring the Kingdom.

THE SHEPHERD FINDS HIS FLOCK—FAITHFULLY

This is the theme Jesus was always coming back to.

"And he spake this parable unto them, saying, What man of you, having a hundred sheep, if he lose one of them . . . doth not go . . . until he find it?" (St. Luke 15.)

Who has not read the classic tale of General Garibaldi leaving for an hour his work for the liberation of Italy to help a shepherd search for a lost lamb? Or who has not brooded long over the thorn-torn figure, arm outstretched over the abyss where vultures scream and circle, reaching for the lost sheep. I do not know which of the great pictures move me most; that, or the one of the little flock lost, piteously lost, in the unrelenting storm, with the wolf upon them.

And who has not stealthily dashed away a tear while the morning soloist sang from the choir-loft,

> "And, all through the mountains, thunder-riven,
> And, up to the rocky steep,
> There arose a glad cry to the gate of heaven,
> 'Rejoice I have found my sheep.'"

Sheep get lost. They move to another town and we either do not know it for months or we do not care enough to notify the shepherd there, to ask his cooperation. Of course, sheep are supposed to tell the shepherd when and where they move. But the pity is, they do not. They are not interested in your job. They do not, all, care that you are interested in them. If they did, they would not be sheep.

Every city is in a constant state of flux. It is no more static than any supposedly solid body is static. Mrs. Jones may live on Main Street, today. She will live in the rear of Brown's

Court next week. No one can keep a church record straight. But it must be attempted. For a church record is living men and women. These are souls.

If attention to the street location were our major problem we might turn the task over to the city directory, the telephone company, the postman, and the polling clerk of the election commission. Each of these will help a new pastor in bringing his roster up to date.

But the finding of sheep is more than this. It involves an uncanny knowledge of sheep psychology. Ol' Mose was asked how he found his master's donkey.

"Well, marse, I jas' says to myse'f, Mose, whah all would you go if you was a donkey. An' I don' gwine thah, and thah he was."

Where are the sheep wandering, these days? Where the pasture looks greenest. They may be deceived. Even animals respond to a mirage. But it is something, to know where to find them.

"And when he hath found it, he layeth it on his shoulders, rejoicing."

THE SHEPHERD FOLDS HIS SHEEP—SAFELY

There is a fold for every flock. There is a den for wild foxes; a pen for domestic animals; a sty for unclean animals; but a fold for safety.

That fold is the Church of God. In that fold the saved soul rests. Within its walls the sheep are fed, protected from the night, and sheltered from the storm. Within the space of five verses Jesus calls himself both the Door and the Shepherd of the fold. Here at this door we stand.

VISITING THE HOMES

In addition to all the calls that one constantly makes, supplemented as these are by the women and the Deacons, the pastor must call on every home in the membership once each year, at a regular time, if he is to serve effectively. The pastor's call is first, simply, an expression of Christian friendship. It may involve finding a parishioner a job, supplying the funds to send a boy to college, or signing a card for the Federal Commissary. It may plunge him into the very middle of a domestic difficulty, or put him to the business of counseling about the rearing of children. Its purpose is acquaintance, sympathy, and the healing of all sense of inferiority on the part of those who think themselves not wanted. Sometimes it seeks to mold opinion but is always patient until opinion is formed. But more than all the rest it is evangelistic in purpose. It is not necessary to be in a home long on this checkup if it is done yearly. Fifty calls per day are entirely possible, if they have been districted. Things to watch for on this checkup are, (1) changes of address. A pastor holding a church is sometimes like a man trying to hold in his hand a handful of flax seed. (2) the neglectful, the careless, the wicked, (3) the disaffected, (4) new born children, (5) new homes established, or about to be established, (6) strangers in the neighborhood who should be attending one's church, (7) those awaiting baptism, (8) the ill, the old, the employed who cannot often attend.

Methods must be devised for reaching the unchurched. A church census conducted in the name of a united Protestantism has value. So has a class in Christian friendliness among the foreign born. Street preaching, and factory meetings at noon, and in the railroad shops, and meetings for women or mothers on Sunday afternoon all have value. All of these agencies take on their greatest value when devoid of overlapping and competition.

THE USHERS

In one's task as a pastor, the ushers are one's greatest asset. The task they perform demands patience, courtesy, tact and a wide knowledge of the congregation. Five people have to do with the success of the public service, pastor, deacons, choir, janitor and, not least, the ushers. A good usher never gets his eye away from the door. He walks *with* the person being shown to a pew; *never* in front. He asks, "What would I want done in this case if I were a pastor." He gets all the congregation forward if possible. But the old and deaf must be shown to the front. He has a pleasant "hand-shake" for those who seem to welcome it. His first law is to maintain quiet and order. His report on attendance is in writing.

An electric button should connect the pastor's office and the pastor's chair with the head usher and a system of signals must be arranged.

My head usher has a card for strangers:

"If after kirk ye bide a wee,
There's some wad like to speak to ye.
If after kirk ye rise and flee,
We'll all seem cold and stiff to ye.
The one that's in the seat with ye,
Is stranger here than ye, maybe.
All here hae got their fears and cares;
Add you your soul unto our prayers,
Be thou our angel unawares."
—*Author unknown.*

THE EVENING SERVICE

The conduct of the evening service is of prime concern. Just now it seems to be slipping badly everywhere. It is always a time for evangelistic preaching. Even though its program may be varied yet its major purpose is always the proclamation of the gospel to the unsaved.

It is well to utilize outside musical talent often. But one will always insist on one's own choir singing an anthem and one's soloist giving a number. And before the evening is over, one mentions the ability and faithfulness of those who assisted. So, is built good will. We cannot compete with any of the amusement enterprises and we will be better off if we do not try. Men who may come to be amused will not come long. Yet this should not be an excuse for dullness. Biography is always interesting. The problems of labor, and crime and poverty and health, and public morality directly relate to the evening service. And ultimately they are the roads that lead to spiritual application.

SPECIAL SERVICES

Special times of refreshing come in almost every church. They are recorded as long ago as in the days of Josiah. (II Kings, Chapter 23.) They are recorded as historic events in the days of Jonah, Ezra, and Elijah.

If they come they have the advantage that they (1) advertise religion in a community; (2) get some to accept of Christ who would not come otherwise; (3) and afford a catharsis of soul for some who wish to reform but have not known how.

They have the disadvantage of burning over the ground so

completely that they make ingathering impossible for a time afterward; and they build a mind-set in some who think that they can come to Christ only "at the next revival."

Conversion may be Pauline in character. But one must never forget Samuel and Timothy.

Pastors will rejoice in special seasons of grace but will not neglect the four ordinary paths of accession.

1. Children in the church and school who come through the school, the pastor's class and decision day.
2. The unsaved in the homes to be won by personal work.
3. The earnest invitation given at the close of many services.
4. The special effort put forth every winter during Lent, in church, and school and by a trained group supplied with names from a carefully prepared prospect list.

It was the shepherds who were watching over their flocks by night to whom the angels came with the announcement of the birth of the Christ Child. So may it be with us who are shepherds of Christ's Kingdom, that we may be found faithfully tending His sheep and guarding them; so that we, too, may go "even unto Bethlehem to see this thing which has come to pass."

BIBLIOGRAPHY

THE great work on the Christian pastor is Practical Theology by J. J. Vanosterzee.

The following additional volumes which can be recommended have been chosen because they offer a wider range and development of the Christian ministry or a specialized treatment of a specific type of ministerial service:

Lectures on Pastoral Theology—Cannon.
Homilitics and Pastoral Theology—Shedd.
For the Gospel Ministry—Blaikie.
The Minister as Shepherd—Jefferson.
The Parish Priest of the Town—Gott.
How to Build a Church—Goodell.
The Christian Pastor and the Working Church—Gladden.
The Christian Pastor in a New Age—Lyman.
Building the Church—Jefferson.
The Experimental Note—Sheridan.
Making Good in the Ministry—Robertson.
New Opportunities—Frederick Lynch.
The Work of the Ministry—Griffith Thomas.
Pastoral Visitation—Savage.
The Priest to the Temple—George Herbert.
Ethics and Etiquette—Henderson.
Outline of Pastoral Theology—Hastie.
The Pastor-Preacher—Quayle.
The Parish—Goodwin.
Prayer and Pastoral Care—Hall.
The Future Leadership of the Church—Mott.

Ethical Dilemmas of the Minister—Mueller and Hartsorn.
The Minister's Job—Palmer.
The Work of the Ministry—Pattison.
The Pastoral Ministry—Adams.
Building a Working Church—Black.
Putting the Church on a Full Time Basis—Beaven.
The Soul Doctor—Zahniser.
The Cure of Souls—MacLaren.
The Cure of Souls—Holman.
The Religion of a Healthy Mind—Holman.
The Christian Ministry—Abbott.
The Parish Priest—Barry and Delaney.
The Pastoral Office—Beebe.
The Making of a Minister—Brown.
The Minister's Week Day Challenge—Byington.
In a Day of Social Rebuilding—Coffin.
The Technique of a Minister—Clausen.
How To Be a Pastor—Cuyler.
Some Problems of the Modern Minister—deBlois.
Pastoral Theology of the New Testament—Beck.
Parish Administration—Fenn.
The Minister and his Parish—Foote.
Maturing in the Ministry—Dolloff.

Date Due

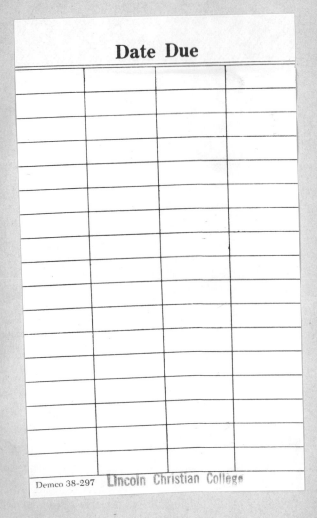